12 Seeds for
Successful
Relationships

Revised & Expanded Edition

BIBLICALLY BASED PRINCIPLES FOR LIFE

12 Seeds for Successful Relationships
Revised and Expanded Edition

First edition: June 2002
Printing of this edition: March 2004
Second printing of this edition: June 2007

Logo design by Keith Gilbert

Cover design by Rick Busch

ISBN: 0-9753844-0-6

Published by
12 Seeds International, Inc.
Minneapolis, MN

We welcome your comments, suggestions, experiences!
Contact us at: comments@12seeds.com
or visit our website at: www.12seeds.com

"We were not born to be alone. God created us for relationship."

– Rebecca Manley Pippert, *Out of the Saltshaker*

The twelve principles presented here, if reviewed periodically and practiced daily, will help you enjoy more excellent relationships in every area of life.

12 *Seeds*™

Contents

Introduction

PART I: The 12 Seeds

PART II: Plant and Cultivate!

PART III: Resources for a Rich Harvest

Introduction

The quality of a person's relationships reflects the quality of a person's life. A person may have good physical health and vast wealth, but if relationships are poor, such a life is not really very healthy or very rich.

What is a family without good relationships? Or a team, a church, a business, or a community? What are friendships without good relationships?

Are you aware that Jesus Christ is very much interested in relationships? He spoke often of them. When He was asked to identify the greatest commandment, His answer had a lot to do with relationships. He said, "Love the Lord your God with all your heart and with all your soul and with all your mind. This is the first and greatest commandment. And the second is like it: Love your neighbor as yourself." Mt 22:37

12 BIBLICALLY BASED PRINCIPLES FOR RELATIONSHIPS

The 12 Seeds are Biblically based principles for building and maintaining relationships based upon love. Some or all of the principles may be familiar to you. However, familiarity with principles is not the primary result we seek. In fact, familiarity may actually keep a person from studying and mastering all twelve.

There are people who assume they understand and know how to practice all of the principles. The truth is that many people are confused about what the principles actually mean and how to apply them in daily life. It's common to encounter people who may think they know about principles like *respect, integrity* and *synergy*, but their behavior suggests otherwise.

The 12 Seeds are not a magic formula for life. Instead, we present them as some of the guiding values that will, when applied in our lives with the Lord's help, produce the full harvest we seek: loving behavior that glorifies the Lord, blesses others, and enriches all of life.

ABOUT THIS BOOK

The purpose of this book is to help you better understand and practice twelve relationship-building principles. We believe that many benefits come to everyone involved when all twelve are learned, reviewed periodically, and practiced daily.

We originally published the 12 Seeds in 2000 as a small pocket-size booklet called *12 Seeds of a Prime Quality Relationship*. In 2001 we revised and reprinted the booklet, adding a Bible verse for each seed. In 2002 we published a larger-size 56-page study book, with the title: *12 Seeds for Growing Relationships*. That book was well received and stimulated engaging discussions in classes and groups. This new revised edition takes the core of that book and expands it with material from discussions and workshops we've led, and from other research.

We hope this book will be a practical guide for you to use throughout your life. Each "seed chapter" in Part I helps you better understand each principle and how to apply it in your life. Each chapter includes a number of practical applications – prayers, thoughts, words, actions, and discussion questions – to help you grow each seed.

Part II further equips you to plant and cultivate the seeds in daily life. It offers practical help to actually grow the seeds. Part III offers additional help in using the twelve seeds for transformational impact in your life with the Lord and with other people.

Our prayer is that you'll reap abundant harvests throughout your life in all your relationships!

"Behold, a sower went forth to sow . . ."

From the Parable of the Sower, Matthew 13:3 KJV

RESPECT
ENCOURAGEMENT
LISTENING
APPRECIATION
TRUST
INTEGRITY
ORDER
NURTURE
SYNERGY
HOPE
IDEALS
PARDON

PART I

The 12 Seeds

Principles for Successful Relationships

Relationship:

A continuing attachment or
association between people who
have dealings with each other;
a dynamic connection between
individuals, or between
an individual and a group.

 12 Seeds™

REGARD, ESTEEM, HONOR

**Honor one another
above yourselves.**
– Romans 12:10

R espect is regard for the existence, ideas and opinions of other people. To respect others is to treat them with dignity and honor. The word "respect" is from the Latin word *respectus,* which means to look at, to regard. Regard, or consideration, is a basic form of respect. Esteem is a higher level of respect, and honor is an even higher level of respect.

Respect involves thinking of others, having consideration for them. It is being thoughtful of others, treating them with courtesy.

OTHER WORDS FOR RESPECT

- attention
- consideration
- deference
- esteem
- honor
- regard

RESPECT: IN OUR RELATIONSHIP WITH THE LORD

Our relationship with the Lord is, of course, the most important relationship we have. In relating to Him there should be a level of respect that goes beyond regard, beyond esteem, beyond honor. The word that describes this highest level of respect is: worship. The Scripture mentions the word "worship" more than 150 times. The dictionary defines worship as "reverent honor, adoring reverence or regard." This highest level of respect should be reserved only for the Lord.

> " . . . this highest level of respect is: worship."

The "fear of the Lord" in the Bible involves this high level of respect. Someone has called the fear of the Lord "supreme respect." The book of Proverbs declares that "The fear of the Lord is the beginning of wisdom." [Pr 9:10] This fear of the Lord, this "supreme respect," is not only a gateway to wisdom, but also to a growing relationship with the Lord.

And as we increasingly consider – *think of* – the Lord, our respect for Him grows into ever greater worship of Him. Our relationship with Him also grows.

We are fortunate that the Lord has regard, a form of respect, for people. In the Old Testament He was constantly thinking of people and interacting with them. In the New Testament He even became human and lived among us. When we look at the life of Jesus, we see Him displaying consideration for everyone. Even while suffering on the cross – *for others* – He asked one of His followers to tend to the needs of His mother.

Besides regard or consideration, the Lord also gives even higher levels of respect to His people. He declares, "This is the one I esteem: he who is humble and contrite in spirit, and trembles at My word." [Is 66:2] And also, "Those who honor Me I will honor." [1Sa 2:30]

RESPECT: IN OUR RELATIONSHIPS WITH OTHERS

Respect is one of the most powerful positive principles in life. Besides being a gateway to our relationship with the Lord, respect is also a gateway to civil relationships with others. In fact, *respect forms the basis for civility in a group and in a society.*

Respect helps meet the human need for *significance.* We all want to feel important, to feel that our lives have meaning, that we count for something. When we respect others, we remind them of these things.

Besides being the gateway to relationships, respect is also the gateway to the practice of the other principles of the 12 Seeds. For example, in order to encourage someone, we first have to have some regard for them: we need to have some thought or consideration of them before we are likely to say or do anything to encourage them.

Respect is a major ingredient in the growth of successful relationships in any family, friendship, group, team, church, business or community.

Symptoms and consequences . . .
HOW TO TELL WHEN RESPECT IS WEAK OR MISSING

In a self-centered world, showing respect for others is often neglected or dismissed. Some people think of respect as just an optional nicety, or an outdated tradition that was forced upon them by people in their past. Others view respect as a social tactic to be used when it serves to advance a personal agenda.

The failure of so many people to grasp the importance of respect and to practice it regularly has brought many tragic consequences for them and for the people around them.

Always make the other person feel important.
– Dale Carnegie

The lack of respect, *dis*respect, is characterized by *dis*regard, *dis*honor, lack of attention, lack of esteem. People tend to ignore one another, acting at times as if others don't even exist. Necessary interactions are uneasy, stressful, even at times confrontational. Rudeness is common. Courtesy is neglected. Politeness is forgotten. People are *inconsiderate*.

Unfortunately, disrespect is a way of life for some people. They know very little about respect. They seldom give it; they seldom receive it. And they may not even realize when they are disrespecting others. Even their humorous little quips and pranks may be thoughtless and disrespectful of others.

Young people sometimes refer to disrespecting or dishonoring a person as "dissing." It has precipitated individual acts of revenge and even gang retaliations. The highway behavior known as "road rage" is probably linked to a disrespect for other people. Disrespect has caused marriages to break up, friendships to dissolve, customers to never return, churches and groups to dwindle, communities to become cold.

Possible reasons . . .
WHY PEOPLE FAIL TO RESPECT

If respect is so important, and the lack of respect so tragic, why don't we give more of it? Let's look at a few of the possible reasons.

First of all, we are by nature self-centered. We tend to think first – sometimes *only* – of ourselves. Also, we fail to follow our Lord's example. We tend to watch the world so much, with its many examples of disrespect, that we take our eyes off the One who was always concerned about people, always thinking of others.

In a world that tends to degrade people it can be easy to regard people as insignificant. We may come to think of them as either nuisances who get in our way, or as tools we can use to further our own interests.

Some people excuse themselves from giving respect because they think that others have not yet met their criteria for deserving or "earning" it. They may feel that how they treat others should be dictated by the way people behave. However, this can lead to a downward spiral of ongoing disrespect.

There are people who, unfortunately, know more ways to disrespect others than they know ways to respect them. These people may have never been taught about respect, or how to practice it. Or, they may have been raised in – or now live and work in – environments where there are no consistent examples of respect being expressed or demonstrated.

The good harvest that results . . .
WHEN RESPECT GROWS

When we respect others, it helps them *feel* important. Even more essential, it reminds them that they *are* important. If the Lord treated people as important and valuable, then so should we. Respecting others can have a dramatic and positive effect upon them, and upon their behavior.

When respect grows, people think more highly and more often of others. People feel cared for and loved. It is said of William Booth, founder of the Salvation Army, that the last word he uttered on his deathbed was "others."

Overall quality of life increases when respect grows. There is a "common courtesy" among people. People are

> **To have respect for ourselves guides
> our morals; and to have deference
> for others governs our manners.**
> – Laurence Sterne

blessed, since respect is a pleasant thing to give and receive. Here's a summary of some of the blessings when respect grows:

- People are reminded that they are significant
- A proper self-image is nourished
- Overall quality of life improves
- Friendships are enhanced
- Other qualities (seeds) are able to grow
- Relationships grow
- Family life improves
- Teams become more effective
- Churches grow in size and effectiveness
- Businesses become more people-oriented
- Communities flourish

And the Lord is worshipped and glorified.

NOTE: The "Practical Applications" section on the next few pages is included in order to provide:
1. examples of practical ways to grow the seed
2. additional material for further study and discussion
3. a "menu" from which you can select specific items that you will add to your own personal practice
Each "seed chapter" includes a similar section.

PRAYER

Some suggestions . . .

> Dear Lord, please help me to have the highest respect for You. Help me to worship You in my thoughts, words and actions.

> Dear Lord, thank You for having regard for people.

> Dear Lord, please help me to treat people with dignity and respect.

THOUGHTS & ATTITUDES

Meditate on Scriptures like these . . .

Exodus 20:12

Proverbs 11:16

Romans 12:10

Romans 13:7

Philippians 2:3

I Peter 2:17

Affirm thoughts like these. . .

- The Lord is great, and worthy of the highest respect! I will worship Him!
- The Lord created people, and He loves them!
- People are important, including me!
- Even when they may appear otherwise, people are important.
- The people around me are important!
- _____ is an important person!
- I will treat _____ with respect!

(Put a person's name in the blanks above)

Other suggestions . . .
- Remember how the Lord respected people.
- Memorize the theme verse at the start of this chapter.
- Think about other people.
- Remember people's names.

WORDS

Suggested things to say or write to others . . .
- "You are important!"
- "_____, I respect your opinion."
- "What do you think, _____?"
- "I've been thinking of you."
- "I'd like to hear your ideas on this."
- "I'd like to know what's important to you."

ACTIONS

Suggestions . . .
- Look at the person who's speaking.
- Hold the door open for others.
- Dress appropriately and respectfully.
- Be on time – respecting a person's time is respecting them.

DISCUSSION

For personal reflection or group consideration . . .

1. What do the Scripture references in the Thoughts & Attitudes section say about respect?

2. Who should we respect? Why?

3. Do I respect others? How?

4. What can I do to show greater respect to others?

5. What will I commit to changing or doing?

INSPIRING WITH COURAGE

> **Let us not give up meeting together,**
> **as some are in the habit of doing, but let us**
> **encourage one another – and all the more**
> **as you see the Day approaching.**
> – Hebrews 10:25

Encouragement is inspiring another person with courage or confidence. It literally means "to give courage to" a person, to reassure them, spur them on, support their efforts to succeed.

To better understand encouragement, let's define two words: courage and inspire. Courage is the state of mind that enables a person to face danger, fear, challenges or unexpected changes with confidence, resolution, bravery. And the word inspire means to stimulate to action, enliven. It's based upon the Latin word *inspirare*, which means "to breathe into."

Therefore, to say that encouragement is "inspiring with courage" is to say that encouragement is stimulating in a person the courage and confidence to face danger, fear, challenges or unexpected changes.

OTHER WORDS FOR ENCOURAGEMENT

- boosting
- cheering
- comforting
- heartening
- motivating
- stimulating

ENCOURAGEMENT: IN OUR RELATIONSHIP WITH THE LORD

From the time Adam sinned,[Ge 3:10] through the Bible to the book of Revelation,[Rev 1:17] we read about how encountering the Almighty God strikes fear in the heart of man. Even His representatives can cause great fear: Luke reports that the shepherds were terrified when the angels announced the birth of Christ.[Lk 2:9]

There are perhaps two types of fear involved when we encounter God. The first is the "fear of the Lord" – the "supreme respect" talked about in the previous chapter. The second type of fear is the intense dread that causes unrighteous people to shrink back in downright speechlessness and paralysis before One who is so holy and mighty and pure.

A very incredible thing is that this Supreme One invites us into a relationship with Himself. Moreover, He encourages us. Though He does require that we keep the "supreme respect" that is due Him, He offers to replace the intense dread with His loving mercy and grace. He even came and walked among us, and wants to befriend us. When He left us for awhile, He provided for our counsel and comfort – He sent His Spirit to live within us, the Holy Spirit, who is called Counselor and Comforter in the Bible.[Jn 14:16-26 see also KJV]

The Lord understands that we face many fears and challenges in life. He encourages us to "fear not." In fact, the phrase "do not be afraid" is used over 65 times in the Bible. Our Lord helps us confront our fears and overcome them. His prayers, His thoughts, His words and His actions are highly encouraging to us.

When we realize that the God of all Creation – the most awesome, powerful Being in the universe – is our friend, then it should put all our fears, however great, in a different perspective. We should indeed be inspired with courage and confidence.

ENCOURAGEMENT: IN OUR RELATIONSHIPS WITH OTHERS

There is much fear today. Modern psychology has identified thousands of different phobias and fears. And what may be fearsome for one person may not be for another. Each person faces their own set of dangers, fears, challenges and unexpected changes in life.

Encouragement helps fill the need people have to face their fears and challenges in life. Relationships can be weakened or strengthened by how people express and respond to those fears and challenges. We can choose to encourage one another, and be encouraged, or we can choose otherwise.

When we consider all that our Lord does for us, and how He encourages us, we should in turn encourage others. Becky Pippert writes of this and offers a paraphrase of the Bible passage that talks about the God who comforts us.[2 Co 1:3-4] Pippert says that we might retranslate the passage this way: "Blessed be the God who has walked alongside of us, who walked alongside of us in our affliction, so that we may be able to walk alongside of others in their affliction with all of the 'walking-alongsidedness' which we have experienced."

Certainly encouragement is one of the finest benefits, one of the most valuable blessings, that people can give one another in their relationships.

Encouragement is oxygen to the soul.
– George M. Adams

Symptoms and consequences . . .

HOW TO TELL WHEN ENCOURAGEMENT IS LACKING

The lack of encouragement, or *dis*couragement, is characterized by a disheartened attitude, lack of motivation, lack of cheer, fear of what may happen, fear of taking risks. Enthusiasm and energy levels are low, and emotional batteries may be drained. People may have little desire to work toward goals that once stimulated them. They may even avoid setting any goals.

Discouraged people tend to focus on problems and worries. Repeated setbacks can dull their resolve. Hopelessness and pessimism may be evident. People may lose their confidence and withdraw in fear and paralysis. Relationships can become difficult and joyless.

Possible reasons . . .

WHY PEOPLE FAIL TO ENCOURAGE OTHERS

Some people fail to encourage others because they fail to realize the great encouragement the Lord offers them. They focus on the discouraging ways of the world rather than the encouraging promises of the Lord. Failing to enjoy the encouragement He offers, they may seek it elsewhere – and their self-centeredness may keep them focused on trying to find encouragement for themselves rather than on giving it to others.

Other people may let the many distractions of life dull their sensitivity to the needs of others. They may forget how greatly everyone needs encouragement. And they may be fooled by the people who mask their fears and pretend they have courage.

Still other people fail to encourage because they lack understanding and skill in doing so. They may forget that different people have different sets of fears and challenges. And they may dismiss certain fears that others have as trivial because they themselves do not have those fears.

Some people fail to encourage others because they live or work in environments where encouragement is seldom given or received. Until someone starts encouraging others, discouragement will prevail.

The good harvest that results . . .
WHEN ENCOURAGEMENT GROWS

People who are encouraged feel that they are not alone in their struggles, that at least one other person notices and cares. Encouragement cheers from the sidelines or even comes alongside in the race.

When a person faces danger, encouragement says, "I'm here with you to help you get through this!" When a person faces fear, encouragement says, "I'm with you to comfort you and help you be brave!" When challenges are faced, encouragement says, "I want you to overcome! I want you to succeed!" When unexpected changes come in life, encouragement says, "I'll help you handle this."

Encouragement to continue on in noble pursuits is a much-needed, highly-welcomed gift we can give to others. It is life-enriching, a perfect gift for all occasions. It yields many blessings. Here are a few of them:
- People are motivated to press on
- A proper self-image is nourished
- People are reassured that others care
- Enthusiasm and energy levels increase
- Efforts are energized and progress continues
- Emotional batteries are recharged
- Friendships are reinforced
- Teamwork grows
- Other qualities (seeds) are stimulated to grow

PRAYER
Some suggestions . . .

Dear Lord, thank You for being the God of encouragement. And thank You for sending Your Holy Spirit to live in me and comfort me.

Dear Lord, thank you for the encouragement You send to me through other people.

Dear Lord, please help me to be sensitive to the dangers, fears, challenges and unexpected changes other people face in life.

Dear Lord, please help me to encourage others, just as You have encouraged me.

THOUGHTS & ATTITUDES
Meditate on Scriptures like these . . .

Joshua 1:1-18

II Samuel 19:7

Psalm 10:17

Isaiah 1:17

Isaiah 41:10

II Corinthians 1:3-4

II Timothy 1:7

Hebrews 10:25

Affirm thoughts like these . . .
- The Lord encourages me!
- The Lord is greater than all my fears!
- The people around me need encouragement.
- _____ needs encouragement.
- I will be an encourager!
- _____ is doing a wonderful job!

Other suggestions . . .
- Meditate on virtually any of the Psalms.
- Memorize the theme verse at the start of this chapter.
- Remember the dangers, fears, challenges and unexpected changes that other people face in life.
- Remember that different people have different sets of fears and challenges.
- Meditate on how the Lord encouraged others.

WORDS
Suggested things to say or write to others . . .
- "Keep up the great work!"
- "_____, I admire your persistence."
- "I know you can do it!"
- "_____, you've put a lot of work into this, and it shows!"
- "Remember what the Lord says in (quote a Bible passage, such as those cited in this chapter)."

If I cannot give my children a perfect mother, I can at least give them more of the one they've got – and make that one more loving. I will be available. I will take time to listen, time to play, time to be home when they arrive from school, time to counsel and encourage.

– Ruth Bell Graham

ACTIONS

Suggestions . . .

- Be sensitive to needs for encouragement – listen to others as they describe what they are facing.
- Take note of the kinds of encouragement that mean the most to the people you're close to.
- Tailor encouragement to the person and their situation.
- Help other people reach their goals.
- Encourage people to practice the 12 Seeds.

DISCUSSION

For personal reflection or group consideration . . .

1. What do the Scripture references in the Thoughts & Attitudes section say about encouragement?

2. What's a good example of encouragement?

3. What could I do to give more encouragement to others?

4. What will I commit to doing?

Have we trials and temptations?
Is there trouble anywhere?
We should never be discouraged,
Take it to the Lord in prayer.
– Joseph Medlicott Scriven

LISTENING

SEEKING TO HEAR, HEEDING

**Everyone should be quick to listen,
slow to speak and slow to become angry.**
– James 1:19b

Listening is "making a conscious effort to hear." It is "paying attention to" another person. Listening involves paying attention to messages that are sent – messages that may be sent in a variety of ways.

Listening includes focusing upon messages sent verbally and also via body language or other means. For example, when we say something like "Listen to your heart," we are referring to a type of listening different from hearing audible sounds. We are really saying, "Pay attention to what your heart is telling you."

Listening goes beyond simply hearing something. Listening involves actually heeding – that is, noticing and considering something – so that it affects a person's thoughts or behavior. Physically hearing a train whistle is only part of listening. Heeding the warning – stopping to let the train pass – is a fuller form of listening that yields a life-saving result.

Even written communication involves listening. For example, if you sent numerous reminders to warn someone, and they failed to heed your warnings, you may refer to the experience by saying, "I tried to warn him, but he just wouldn't listen to me."

OTHER WORDS FOR LISTENING

- attending
- considering
- hearkening
- heeding

LISTENING: IN OUR RELATIONSHIP WITH THE LORD

Listening to the Lord is one of the most important – and wisest – things that we humans can ever do. The Bible uses the word "listen" 352 times, and many of those uses are admonitions to listen to the Lord. In many cases He is giving warnings that a wise person would heed; in other cases He is pointing out something that we should understand.

We could say that the entire Bible is something we should be listening to, because God is speaking to us there. We need to listen to His voice. The importance of this is illustrated in the story of the young apprentice priest Samuel. The elderly priest Eli instructed Samuel to respond to the Lord's call in this way: "Speak, LORD, for your servant is listening." [1 Sa 3:9]

In later years, the Lord Himself commended Mary for listening to Him,[Lk 10:39-42] while her sister Martha was busy fussing with less important things.

A wonderful thing in our relationship with the Lord is the fact that He also listens to us. David pleaded, "Hear my cry, O God; listen to my prayer. From the ends of the earth I call to You, I call as my heart grows faint; lead me to the rock that is higher than I."[Ps 61:1-2] And He – the great God of the Universe – has promised to answer us, as He assured the prophet Jeremiah: "Call to me and I will answer you and tell you great and unsearchable things you do not know." [Jer 33:3] As He tells us those things, what an awesome time to be listening!

LISTENING: IN OUR RELATIONSHIPS WITH OTHERS

Listening is, of course, also highly important in all human relationships. It is foundational to good communication. When someone sends messages, with no one paying attention or making an effort to receive those messages, communication has not occurred. Listening makes communication possible. And communication, everyone agrees, is essential for relationships.

Listening helps fill our need for attention. From infancy we're always crying out for attention – some of us more than others. Listening helps give people the attention they need.

And there's another major reason why listening is so important: *we learn when we listen*. It is through listening that we learn important things we need to know in life. It is through listening that we get to know other people, and learn about their fears, needs and dreams.

Symptoms and consequences . . .
HOW TO TELL WHEN LISTENING IS WEAK OR MISSING

When people fail to listen to one another, relationships seldom grow. Misunderstandings are frequent, teamwork is poor, mistakes are common. People may be so focused on what they want to say that they take little or no time to listen to messages being sent by other people. Insensitivity to others may prevail. People may be emotionally distant from one another.

When listening is lacking, people ignore others, children don't pay attention to their parents, individuals fail

The first duty of love is to listen.
– Paul Tillich

to heed safety warnings, and people who are blessed with resources fail to hear the cries of the needy.

Since listening is part of being teachable, when listening is lacking learning is virtually impossible. This is a major reason why poor listeners fail to know and understand other people.

Possible reasons...
WHY PEOPLE FAIL TO LISTEN

Self-centeredness is a big reason why people fail to listen. We can be so focused on what we're thinking or want to say that we fail to listen to others. And we forget that people need attention. Also, listening can be hard work. There are some who think listening is a waste of time, and there are others who don't listen because they don't really know how. They may be good at sending messages, but poor at receiving them.

The good harvest that results...
WHEN LISTENING GROWS

When listening grows, people receive the attention they need. They are able to express themselves, and voice their fears, needs, joys and dreams. People show they care about others when they listen, and are willing to invest time to be with them. The gift of listening is a gift that another person may treasure for a lifetime. To summarize some of the benefits of listening:

- People receive the attention they need
- People feel respected and encouraged
- Effective communication increases
- Learning occurs
- Interpersonal understanding increases
- Miscues and mistakes decrease
- Teamwork improves
- Healing can take place
- Relationships grow

PRAYER

Some suggestions . . .

> Dear Lord, help me to always listen to You.
>
> Dear Lord, thank You for listening to me.
>
> Dear Lord, help me to be a better listener to the people around me.

THOUGHTS & ATTITUDES

Meditate on Scriptures like these . . .

> I Samuel 3:10
>
> Proverbs 18:13
>
> Proverbs 19:27
>
> Jeremiah 7:2
>
> Acts 16:25
>
> James 1:19

Affirm thoughts like these . . .

- People need to be heard!
- I need to be quiet once in awhile and listen.
- I can learn from others.
- I want to hear what _____ has to say.
- _____ is worth listening to.

Other suggestions . . .

- Read the Bible to hear God speaking to you.
- Think about the messages people send you.
- Remember that listening is a gift you can give.
- Focus on the meaning being conveyed.

A good listener is not only popular everywhere, but after a while he knows something.

– Misner

WORDS

Suggested things to say or write to others . . .

- "Thanks for telling me that!"
- "Tell me more!"
- "How are you, *really*?"
- "You express yourself well!"
- "Thanks for listening!"
- "I always learn when I listen to you!"
- "Let me repeat back to you what I heard you say."

ACTIONS

Suggestions . . .

- Look at the person who is speaking.
- Actively listen – note tone of voice, body language, speed of delivery, facial expressions, use of descriptive words.
- Take notes.
- Be patient. Listen well before responding.

DISCUSSION

For personal reflection or group consideration . . .

1. What do the Scripture references in the Thoughts & Attitudes section say about listening?

2. Who should we listen to? Why?

3. What's a good example of listening?

4. What could I do in order to do a better job of giving the gift of listening to others?

5. What will I commit to doing?

**We have two ears and only one tongue in order
that we may hear more and speak less.**
– Diogenes

GRATEFUL RECOGNITION OF VALUE

**Be joyful always; pray continually;
give thanks in all circumstances, for
this is God's will for you in Christ Jesus.**
– 1 Thessalonians 5:16-18

Appreciation is grateful recognition of the value, quality or significance of a gift, deed or person. The word "appreciation" is based upon the Latin *appretaire,* meaning "to appraise."

Appreciation is the expression of gratitude. It is acknowledging the value of someone or something, and then expressing thankfulness for it. It can include praising someone for something they have done.

OTHER WORDS FOR APPRECIATION
- acknowledgment
- gratitude
- recognition
- thankfulness

APPRECIATION: IN OUR RELATIONSHIP WITH THE LORD

Whenever we come into a fuller understanding of the goodness and mercy of the Lord, the reaction has to include appreciation for Him – who He is and what He has done and is doing. It is certainly an important part of our worship of the Lord and of our expression of praise to Him.

How we look at things, our attitudes and our worldview, has a lot to do with how much appreciation we express to the Lord. If we think we're the center of the universe, and everything revolves around us, then it's unlikely we'll express much gratitude to the Lord.

On the other hand, if we acknowledge the Lord as the awesome Creator of the universe, the All-powerful One, then this recognition of His great value will stimulate appreciation. We'll join with the Psalmist when he exclaims, "Praise the LORD. Praise God in his sanctuary; praise Him in His mighty heavens. Praise Him for his acts of power; praise Him for his surpassing greatness." Ps. 150:1-2 In addition, when we realize that the Lord loves us and values us, our hearts should overflow in still greater praise to Him!

When we study the Lord and live in a relationship with Him, we come to realize that He also appreciates people who honor and serve Him. For example, He gave recognition to His servant Job when He said: "There is no one on earth like him; he is blameless and upright, a man who fears God and shuns evil." Job 1:8b

God's love for us shows how much He values us. Sending His Son makes that clear. We in turn should respond with everlasting appreciation to Him. We have so much to thank Him for!

APPRECIATION: IN OUR RELATIONSHIPS WITH OTHERS

In addition to being important in our relationship with the Lord, appreciation is of great importance in our relationships with others. People need acknowledgment that they – and the things they do – are valued. Appreciation tells them they are. Appreciation gives people positive feedback. It affirms worthy performance and encourages more of it.

Appreciation is important not only because people need to receive it, but because when a person's heart is full of gratitude, they need to give it. Giver and receiver are both blessed.

Symptoms and consequences . . .
HOW TO TELL WHEN APPRECIATION IS WEAK OR MISSING

Often referred to as "ingratitude," the lack of appreciation means that people don't receive positive feedback when they do things or give things of value. They may be discouraged from doing more, or unmotivated to press on. When appreciation is lacking, people feel their efforts are ignored, their contributions wasted. Even worse, they may come to feel that they themselves are not valued for who they are.

When appreciation is weak or missing, we hear people say things like, "They don't appreciate what I do." "She's so ungrateful." "He never gives anybody any credit."

Possible reasons . . .
WHY PEOPLE FAIL TO APPRECIATE

Pride is a big reason we fail to appreciate others. We are so focused upon ourselves that we fail to value others and what they do. At times we don't even realize all the things others give to us and do for us.

We forget to thank the Lord for His provision in our lives, and instead think we've earned whatever we have. We forget to recognize the people that the Lord sends to minister to our many needs. And we forget that people are valuable and precious to the Lord – and that they should be to us as well.

Gratitude is the memory of the heart.
– Jean Baptiste Massieu

Some people fail to appreciate what others do because they may not like to admit that they ever have any needs. Or, they don't want to acknowledge that other people have helped them.

Some people think that expressing thanks is only an optional politeness. Others fail to express gratitude because they think they don't have the time to say thanks, which is ironic, since someone took the time to give.

There are people who grew up in environments where appreciation was seldom given or received. They never learned how to practice it. They need to learn from the practices of the Lord Jesus, who always gave thanks to His Father.

The good harvest that results . . .
WHEN APPRECIATION GROWS

When appreciation grows, people feel valued. They sense that their presence and their efforts are acknowledged and have significance. Friendships grow warmer. Appreciation brings a harvest of good feelings and blessings to any relationship and to any environment. Among the many blessings:
- People feel valued
- People feel that what they do gets noticed
- People receive positive feedback
- Fear of failure decreases
- Positive behavior is reinforced
- Gratitude displaces greed
- The abilities and gifts people have are affirmed
- Joy increases
- Teamwork improves
- People are motivated
- Relationships are brightened

No duty is more urgent than that of returning thanks.
– Ambrose of Milan

PRAYER

Some suggestions . . .

> Dear Lord, thank You for who
> You are and what You do.

> Dear Lord, please help me to better express my
> appreciation and gratitude to You.

> Dear Lord, help me to be more grateful to others
> for who they are and for what they do.

THOUGHTS & ATTITUDES

Meditate on Scriptures like these . . .

Psalm 100:4

Matthew 14:19

I Corinthians 15:57

Ephesians 5:20

I Thessalonians 1:2

I Thessalonians 5:16-18

Affirm thoughts like these . . .

- I appreciate the people around me!
- I'm so thankful!
- I appreciate what others do for me.
- _____ is a blessing in my life.
- The Lord values me!

Other suggestions . . .

- Read the Psalms.
- Remember what the Lord has done for you.
- Remember what other people have done for you.
- Remember who you are in Christ.

WORDS

Suggested things to say or write to others . . .

- "Thanks for helping me!"
- "I appreciate you so much!"
- "_____, thanks!"
- "Thanks for being here!"
- "I'd like to tell you what _____ did for me."

ACTIONS

Suggestions . . .

- Send a thank-you note or e-mail.
- Recognize the character qualities of others.
- Recognize achievements of others.
- Watch for people doing praiseworthy things.
- Give awards.

DISCUSSION

For personal reflection or group consideration . . .

1. What do the Scripture references in the Thoughts & Attitudes section say about appreciation?

2. Think of a time you received appreciation. How was it expressed? How did it make you feel?

3. Do you let others know how much you appreciate them, and the things they do for you? How?

4. What could you do to show more appreciation?

5. What will you commit to doing?

**How happy a person is depends upon
the depth of his gratitude.**

– John Miller

CONFIDENCE IN ANOTHER

**Trust in the LORD with all your heart
and lean not on your own understanding;
in all your ways acknowledge Him, and
He will make your paths straight.**

– Proverbs 3:5-6

Trust is firm belief or confidence in the honesty, integrity or reliability of another person or thing. Total trust should only be placed in God; limited levels of trust may be placed in others. Though trust takes time to develop, it's essential for relationships.

OTHER WORDS FOR TRUST

- belief
- confidence
- faith
- reliance

TRUST: IN OUR RELATIONSHIP WITH THE LORD

Trust, or faith, is of prime importance to the Lord. The Old Testament uses the word "trust" 79 times and the word "faith" 16 times, while the New Testament uses "trust" 10 times and "faith" 254 times.

The Bible declares that "without faith it is impossible to please God." [Heb 11:6] Moses learned this the hard way. Even though he was in a very close relationship with the Lord, he did something that displeased the Lord. The Lord said to Moses, "Because you did not trust in me enough to honor me as holy in the sight of the Israelites, you will not bring this community into the land I give them." Nu 20:12b

Trust is serious business to the Lord. Our trust in Him is to be complete: "Trust in the LORD with all your heart . . ." Pr 3:5-6 It includes surrender to His lordship and His trustworthiness. It is having total confidence in Him as the only One in the universe who is worthy of our complete trust.

Does the Lord trust us? An answer: "Yes, to a point." The Bible says that Jesus would not entrust Himself to the people who were following Him, because He knew what was in the heart of man." Jn 2:24-25 And yet, we know that He entrusts us with some of His resources, and He reminds us that as stewards we are to be found faithful and trustworthy.1 Co 4:2 He even entrusts us to carry His Good News, the Gospel, to others.2 Ti 2:2 And as we follow Him, we become more trustworthy.

TRUST: IN OUR RELATIONSHIPS WITH OTHERS

Trust enables people to develop and maintain friendships. A basic level of trust is needed for any relationship. Greater levels are required for close relationships to develop and grow. We exercise some level of trust in virtually every interaction we have with other people. For example, there is the level of trust we have when we let a mechanic service our car; there is the trust we have in an employer or in a buyer to pay for the services or goods we are providing.

Trust helps fill our need for security. Relationships that offer such security grow deeper and provide blessings for each person involved.

We must be careful, however, that trust is not misplaced. We should not expect the complete trustworthiness of people that can be found only in the Lord.

Symptoms and consequences . . .
HOW TO TELL WHEN TRUST IS WEAK OR MISSING

The lack of trust, *dis*trust, means that people don't have confidence in one another. They're suspicious of others and unwilling to rely upon one another. Working together can be difficult, stressful, often unproductive. Second-guessing, or the fear of it, wastes energies and hampers progress. Masks and evasive tactics may hide true feelings and needs from one another.

When trust is lacking, people are unwilling to rely upon the strengths of others, thus teamwork suffers or never develops at all. People may attack one another rather than the challenges at hand. Friendships are frail, often unable to endure the trials that inevitably come. People may feel detached and alone.

Worry can be overwhelming when trust is lacking.

Possible reasons . . .
WHY PEOPLE FAIL TO TRUST

Perhaps the underlying reason people fail to trust others is that they don't have a firm trust in the Lord. They may be looking for ultimate security in people, who of course cannot provide it. As they try to place complete faith in people, they are repeatedly disappointed and trust others less and less.

Some people have sad experiences of trusting others in the past, people who proved untrustworthy. They were hurt deeply. They don't want to be hurt again. So they simply do not trust other people for much of anything.

Other people won't trust because they want to be self-sufficient and independent from others. They want to avoid having to rely upon other people. Still others simply have a skeptical, questioning nature. It's part of their makeup to ask questions and even to second-guess. Carried too far, this can prevent the growth of trust in a relationship as the other person comes to feel that everything he or she does will be questioned.

Then of course there are some people who are quite untrustworthy themselves. Trust is not part of their lives: they don't give it, and they don't receive it.

The good harvest that results . . .
WHEN TRUST GROWS

When complete trust is placed in the Lord, a person rests upon the faithfulness of the One who said He would always be with us.[Mt 28:20] With our complete trust anchored in Him, we are free to place a proper level of trust in other people.

As trust grows between people in a relationship, they no longer have the need to continually question each other's motives. Increased trust brings forth greater levels of meaning as they're able to share their fears, needs, joys and dreams at increasing levels of significance. Many people consider trusted friends as their greatest treasures in life. Other benefits include:

- People are able to confide in one another
- Wasteful time and energy spent maintaining masks and evasive tactics decreases
- People learn interesting new things about each other, including strengths and weaknesses
- People work together more effectively
- Micromanagement decreases
- People learn to take on increased responsibility
- Teamwork grows
- Other seeds can grow
- Friendships grow

PRAYER
Some suggestions...

> Dear Lord, please help me to
> trust in You completely.

> Dear Lord, please help me to
> wisely trust other people.

> Dear Lord, please help me to be trustworthy.

THOUGHTS & ATTITUDES
Meditate on Scriptures like these...

Psalm 34:8 (esp. KJV)

Psalm 40:4

Proverbs 3:5,6

Proverbs 29:25

Proverbs 31:10,11

I Corinthians 4:1,2

Affirm thoughts like these...
- In God We Trust.
- I trust _____.
- Our trust level is increasing.
- Trust is precious and deserves careful handling.

Other suggestions...
- Trust completely in God.
- Trust wisely and carefully in others.

**Be courteous to all, but intimate with few; and let those
few be well tried before you give them your confidence.**
– George Washington

WORDS

Suggested things to say or write to others . . .

- "_____, I trust you."
- "You are a trustworthy friend."
- "I will honor the trust you have in me."

ACTIONS

Suggestions . . .

- Venture out of your comfort zone.
- Delegate or share the workload.
- Avoid micromanaging others.
- Be patient.

DISCUSSION

For personal reflection or group consideration . . .

1. What do the Scripture references in the Thoughts & Attitudes section say about trust?

2. Whom should we trust? Why?

3. Does trust have various levels?

4. What's a good example of trust?

5. What could I do to give more trust to others?

6. What will I commit to doing?

> **It is an equal failing to trust everybody,
> and to trust nobody.**
> – 18th Century English Proverb

> **Society is built upon trust, and trust upon
> confidence in one another's integrity.**
> – Robert South

INTEGRITY

MORAL STRENGTH & WHOLENESS

The integrity of the upright guides them, but the unfaithful are destroyed by their duplicity.
— Proverbs 11:3

Integrity is from the Latin *integritas,* which means "soundness, purity," and *integer,* "whole, complete." In mathematics, a whole number is called an integer, as opposed to a fraction.

Integrity is steadfast adherence to a moral or ethical code. It is the condition of being sound, complete, integrated. With integrity, one's thoughts, words and actions all agree with each other.

OTHER WORDS FOR INTEGRITY

- character
- ethics
- fidelity
- honor
- honesty
- soundness
- virtue
- wholeness

INTEGRITY: IN OUR RELATIONSHIP WITH THE LORD

Integrity is essential in a growing relationship with the Lord. Jesus is the perfect model of integrity: He is "real" with us; He expects us to "be real" with Him.

Our relationship with the Lord is unlike any other. One of the unique things about it is that He knows us inside and out. We can't get away with hiding anything from Him. Coverups didn't work for Adam and Eve back in the Garden of Eden, and they certainly don't work for us today. The Bible declares, "Nothing in all creation is hidden from God's sight. Everything is uncovered and laid bare before the eyes of Him to whom we must give account."[Heb 4:13]

One of the things Jesus hates most is hypocrisy, which is the practice of professing beliefs, feelings or virtues that one does not actually hold or possess. Essentially, it's a lack of integrity, and He warned His followers to be on guard against it.[Lk 12:1] Jesus hated to see people appearing righteous on the outside when they were evil on the inside.[Mt 23:28]

Integrity involves a proper handling of truth, and truth is of high importance to the Lord. The Bible uses the word "truth" 41 times in the Old Testament, 183 times in the New. Remember, Jesus identified Himself as being "the Way, the Truth, and the Life."[Jn 14:6]

There are other aspects of integrity involved in our relationship with the Lord: health and well-being. It's interesting that in the story of the healing of a man with a withered hand, the Bible says that the hand "was completely restored, just as sound as the other."[Mt 12:13] In another translation, the Bible says that the hand was made "whole."[Mt 12:13 KJV] The story associates healing with restoration of soundness and wholeness, which are definitions of integrity.

INTEGRITY: IN OUR RELATIONSHIPS WITH OTHERS

Integrity is essential if relationships are to be strong. Both in business and in personal life, integrity is one of the most highly valued character qualities. It invites trust, and helps trust grow.

Integrity helps fill the human need for authenticity. We all want people to be real with us. We want the genuine article. We hate to be lied to. We want the truth. We want people to be honest and open with us.

There's another aspect of integrity in our relationship with other believers: integration, which means "to make one." Jesus hates to see His followers divided. In one of His recorded prayers He requested three times that His followers "may be one." ^{Jn 17:11-22}

Symptoms and consequences . . .
HOW TO TELL WHEN INTEGRITY IS WEAK OR MISSING

When integrity is lacking, a person's thoughts, words and actions don't line up. People say one thing, and do something else. They lie and mislead.

When integrity is lacking, there's a state of disintegration, where things are coming apart. It is a state of "dis" integrity. In this state people "go to pieces," relationships "fall apart," trust is "broken."

Without integrity, relationships are unsound, unwhole, incomplete. People hurt one another, whether they mean to or not. People deceive and are deceived. The consequences are painful. Trust fails to grow, and other seeds suffer also. It's a devastating way to live.

Possible reasons . . .
WHY PEOPLE FAIL TO PRACTICE INTEGRITY

Some people forget that we all stand before an Almighty God who knows our every thought, hears our every word, and sees our every action. They forget that we are accountable to Him.

Another reason people fail at integrity is that their self-centeredness makes them resistant to any reality or set of morals other than what's expedient for their own selfish gain. This is a type of self-deception, practiced by people who are afraid to deal with the truth.

Some people foolishly think that being cleverly deceitful shows that they're smarter than other people. Or they may think that the end justifies the means. Some are running with the wrong crowd. Still others have never learned what integrity actually is.

It's easy to neglect integrity when news reports so frequently focus on people who don't have it. Also, some segments of our modern culture do little to teach about integrity or how to practice it.

The good harvest that results . . .
WHEN INTEGRITY GROWS

When integrity grows, relationships grow more healthy and sound. People don't seek to deceive others, and are less likely to be deceived themselves. People face reality. They're "real" with one another.

When integrity grows, people focus more on what the Lord considers right, rather than the current popular opinion. They look to Jesus as the model for perfect integrity. And they rejoice when integrity is practiced in the lives of other people.

Integrity brings refreshing simplicity. Life can be complicated enough without having to deal with people who are two-faced. A list of some benefits of integrity:
- Time and effort don't have to be wasted in hiding motives, covering tracks or making up excuses
- Less injury is done to others
- Life gets simpler, and stress decreases
- We can be more devoted to positive things rather than to recovering from the negatives of deceit
- Teamwork and progress improves
- People do what they said they would do
- Trusting relationships grow

PRAYER

Some suggestions . . .

> Dear Lord, please help me to have integrity in Your eyes.

> Dear Lord, please help my thoughts, words and actions to all be in agreement.

> Dear Lord, please help me to have integrity in all my relationships with others.

THOUGHTS & ATTITUDES

Meditate on Scriptures like these . . .

Psalm 26:1-5

Psalm 139:23,24

Proverbs 10:9

Proverbs 11:3-5

Mark 12:14

I Peter 2:12

Affirm thoughts like these . . .

- I will not deceive others.
- Integrity is a quality that I highly value.
- Honesty is the best policy.
- _____ is a person of integrity.

WORDS

Suggested things to say or write to others . . .

- "What is the right way to do this?"
- "Please help me sort out my motives."
- "I admire your integrity."
- "Thanks for being honest with me."
- "What would Jesus want us to do now?"

Other suggestions . . .
- Tell the truth.
- Don't spread gossip or rumors.
- Say clearly what you mean.

ACTIONS

Suggestions . . .
- Do what you said you would do.
- Study people who have integrity, learn from them.
- Focus on the truth, acknowledge the facts.
- Do the right thing, maintain high standards.
- Practice integrity in small as well as large things.
- Get into an accountability relationship.

DISCUSSION

For personal reflection or group consideration . . .

1. What do the Scripture references in the Thoughts & Attitudes section say about integrity?

2. What's a good example of integrity?

3. What are signs that greater integrity is needed?

4. What could I do to practice greater integrity?

5. What will I commit to doing?

Character is what you are in the dark.
– Dwight L. Moody

**People may doubt what you say,
but they will always believe what you do.**
– Anonymous

ORDER

STRUCTURE, PRIORITIES, GUIDELINES

**Everything should be done in a
fitting and orderly way.**

– 1 Corinthians 14:40

O rder is arrangement of the parts of a whole. It includes observance of law and civil conduct. In a relationship it includes guidelines and boundaries for conduct, as well as agreement on *priorities*. Priorities are the "prior order" of importance or precedence.

Practicing orderly behavior is called discipline. It's characterized by good habits and profitable routines.

OTHER WORDS FOR ORDER

- discipline
- harmony
- orderliness
- pattern
- routine
- structure

ORDER: IN OUR RELATIONSHIP WITH THE LORD

When we look to the Lord we see His structure and design in the universe He created – there's an amazing order throughout His Creation. We also see incredible order in His detailed design for both the Tabernacle and the Temple in the Old Testament. He most certainly is concerned with order and structure.

The Lord is also very concerned about priorities. This is revealed when He was asked about which commandment was the greatest. He responded by declaring that the greatest was to love God. The second greatest commandment, He said, was to love your neighbor as yourself.[Mk 12:28-31] As we study the life of Christ, we see Him following this order, this set of priorities, in His life.

Guidelines are also important in our relationship with the Lord. His guidelines are so perfect that He calls them laws. His laws reveal His ways. As we come to understand more about Him and about His ways, our appreciation grows to the point where we can exclaim with the psalmist, "Oh, how I love your law! I meditate on it all day long." [Ps 119:97]

As we learn from Him about His laws, we learn more about how things actually work, including relationships. And we find help in developing excellent structure, priorities and guidelines for our lives. We learn how to please Him, while also discovering that His order is the best way for us to live.

ORDER: IN OUR RELATIONSHIPS WITH OTHERS

Order is needed for individuals to live and work well together. Order is the structure that enables groups to attain quality conditions and achievements that benefit all. Order encompasses the priorities – shared and individual – that direct efforts. And it is the set of guidelines and boundaries that help people live and work together in peace.

The need for order is one of the primary reasons for the entire system of law and its enforcement in a society. Civilized people want to maintain law and *order.*

Symptoms and consequences . . .
HOW TO TELL WHEN ORDER IS WEAK OR MISSING

Called *dis*order, the lack of order takes many forms: a disorganized life, confused priorities, lawlessness. In lesser ways, the absence of order can be evident in a disorderly room, a messy garage, lack of punctuality.

When order is lacking, efforts are unorganized and priorities may never even be established. Discipline may be mocked, boundaries ignored, commitments neglected. Rules may be observed only when convenient. Laws are broken, and anarchy may prevail. Fights or riots may even break out.

An example of disorder would be an uncontrolled traffic intersection where drivers behave as though they each have the right of way and can proceed as fast as they wish. The resulting injury and damage would be painful reminders of the consequences of disorder.

Possible reasons . . .
WHY PEOPLE FAIL TO PRACTICE ORDER

Ever since Adam and Eve chose to rebel and not follow the Lord's instructions, we humans have wanted to do things our own way. We want what we want when we want it, without regard for the impact on others. We tend to dislike being accountable to rules or standards.

Some people are simply unwilling to invest the time and effort order requires. Others never learned how to organize. They may be, as one person put it, "organizationally challenged." Still others may erroneously think that order restricts rather than frees a person.

People will at times neglect order when they forget the many negative consequences of what is eager to take over in their lives: disorder.

Lack of effective leadership can be a major factor in the neglect of order. A leader should coordinate the mutual efforts of people to achieve a shared goal or objective. Coordination (*think* "co-order") is a major part of order. Every leader should promote order, and should personally be a good role model for orderly behavior and a commitment to discipline.

The good harvest that results . . .
WHEN ORDER GROWS

While some people say they want complete freedom to do whatever they wish, only the very foolish want to live without order. The desire for law and order prompts people to put up stop signs, set driving laws, and establish other rules to help people live together in safety.

Order also brings basic guidelines for relationships, priorities to direct our efforts, and streamlined routines to get tasks done efficiently.

Wise people find that ordering their lives according to the Lord's principles grants them freedom and joy in life. They're thankful that a loving Lord has inspired guidelines to be recorded in His book for living a successful, orderly life with one another. A few of the many benefits of order:

- People interrelate with civility
- People have a track to run on
- Many destructive behaviors and their consequences can be avoided
- Individual schedules coordinate better
- Resources are employed more effectively
- Tasks get done more efficiently as orderly habits and routines are practiced and refined

**Unless you have a strong, healthy routine,
I doubt that you can live a successful life.**
– Dave Thomas

PRAYER

Some suggestions . . .

> Dear Lord, please help me to better understand and live by the order You have created.

> Dear Lord, please help me better understand what's important to You.

> Dear Lord, please help me to live an orderly life that will be a blessing to people around me.

THOUGHTS & ATTITUDES

Meditate on Scriptures like these . . .

> Psalm 119:133

> Proverbs 15:32

> Proverbs 28:2

> I Corinthians 14:40

Affirm thoughts like these . . .

- Discipline brings many benefits!
- Routines conserve mental energy!

Other suggestions . . .

- Frequently ask yourself: "What is most important?"
- Learn the rules.
- Think of rules as guidelines for orderly living.
- Identify and focus on top priorities.

Discipline is demanded of the athlete to win a game. Discipline is required for the captain running his ship. Discipline is needed for the pianist to practice for the concert. Only in the matter of personal conduct is the need for discipline questioned.

– Gladys Brooks

WORDS

Suggested things to say or write to others . . .

- "Thanks for helping me organize this!"
- "What's important here?"
- "How do you get things done so efficiently?"
- "Please help me clarify my priorities."

ACTIONS

Suggestions . . .

- Keep priorities in writing, reread them often.
- Watch people who are organized – learn from them.
- Develop routines for necessary tasks.
- Simplify, clarify, eliminate clutter.
- Get into an accountability relationship – hold one another accountable to good habits and disciplines.

DISCUSSION

For personal reflection or group consideration . . .

1. What do the Scripture references in the Thoughts & Attitudes section say about order?

2. What are some signs that greater order may be needed in our lives?

3. How does the level of order in my life affect my relationships?

4. What's a good example of order?

5. What could I do to practice greater order in my life and in my relationships?

6. What will I commit to doing?

NURTURE

CARE & FEEDING, LOVING SUPPORT

Love never fails.
– 1 Corinthians 13:8a

Nurture is caring for someone, providing help and nutrition to promote their welfare and development. Closely related to the word "love," nurture is love in action. It is doing things for the welfare of others. Nurture is the way we apply all 12 Seeds for the benefit of others.

OTHER WORDS FOR NURTURE
- assistance
- care
- comfort
- nourishment

NURTURE: IN OUR RELATIONSHIP WITH THE LORD

Our Lord nurtures people. To look at His life while He walked among us is to see a person who was constantly caring for others. He fed them. He healed them.

The parables He told, like the story of the Good Samaritan,[Lk 10:25-37] clearly reveal His love for people. His great love for people is of course a great benefit for us as we live in a relationship with Him – we are the recipients of His abiding love. He cares about our worries: the Bible urges us to "Cast all your anxiety on Him because He cares for you." [1Pe 5:7] He cares for our major needs, such as salvation: "For God so loved . . ." [Jn 3:16] and also for our everyday needs, like daily bread. [Mt 6:11]

He also cares that we learn His ways. Such training is part of our nurture. It's notable that where one Bible translation refers to the "training and instruction of the Lord," [Eph 6:4] another translation calls it the "nurture and admonition of the Lord." [Eph 6:4 KJV]

Nurture in our relationship with the Lord is two-way, because He also allows us to care for Him. When He walked among us, people followed Him "to care for his needs." [Mt 27:55] And before He left us, He told us we were to show our love for Him in the way we cared for others. After He returned to heaven, we would no longer be able to show our love for Him by directly caring for Him, but if we truly loved Him we would show it by caring for others. He went so far as to say that, at the Final Judgment, He will declare, "whatever you did for one of the least of these brothers of mine, you did for me." [Mt 25:40]

NURTURE: IN OUR RELATIONSHIPS WITH OTHERS

It could be argued that people who have obeyed the Lord's commands to love others have done more for the welfare of other people on this earth than have the followers of any other teacher in history. We will not try to defend this assertion here, but will simply say that nurture for others should overflow into all of our relationships if we love the Lord and obey Him.

We must remember that our Lord loves people, not because they deserve it, but because love is an essential part of His nature. [1 Jn 4:16] And love should be an essential part of our nature too. We can be a channel of His love to other people, just as they often are to us.

We all need to be cared for, whether we realize it or not. One of the beautiful characteristics of healthy relationships is that people help meet the needs of one another – that is, they nurture one another. Each person has various gifts and needs. Each shares their gifts to meet the needs of others.

It's interesting that when we care for the welfare of others – when we love them – our Lord notices. He is especially concerned for the poor among us, people who are needy in spirit or needy in resources. In fact, Proverbs says that the Lord will repay the kindness we show to needy people.[Pr 19:17]

Symptoms and consequences . . .
HOW TO TELL WHEN NURTURE IS WEAK OR MISSING

When nurture is lacking, people care only about themselves and not the needs of others. People feel isolated, lonely, neglected. The closeness that develops when people help and are helped is missing. People with needs they cannot fill limp through life, crippled in reaching their potential. And people with gifts they could share hoard those gifts and miss the joy that comes in helping others.

Possible reasons . . .
WHY PEOPLE FAIL TO NURTURE

Self-centeredness and pride are major reasons why people fail to care for others. Some people are so caught up in getting all they can get in life that they have little time or energy left to look to the needs of others. Sometimes, they don't even see the needs. At other times they say they're too busy to get involved.

You can give without loving,
but you cannot love without giving.
– Amy Carmichael

Some people don't nurture others because love is often inconvenient. It takes time, energy and other resources. Other people put off caring for others until they themselves are given more time, energy and resources.

Sometimes people fail to nurture because they forget that everyone needs help of some kind. Or, they may not realize how valuable the help they're able to give can be to others in need.

People who fail to care for others are disobeying our Lord's command, and they're forgetting that in loving others they're showing love to the Lord.

The good harvest that results . . .
WHEN NURTURE GROWS

When nurture grows, needs are filled. People feel cared for, and they are cared for. People come to realize the joys of giving and receiving help. They come to realize that "we need each other."

As our understanding grows, we find that many, perhaps most, of God's gifts come through other people. Each of us can be an instrument by which others are blessed. Here are some of the blessings when nurture grows:
- People get the help they need
- People experience the joy of helping others
- Skills are put to worthy use
- Resources are put to worthy use
- Other-centeredness replaces self-centeredness
- People grow
- Relationships are strengthened
- The Lord is pleased as we show our love for Him in the way we love others

If we could read the secret history of our enemies, we should find in each man's life sorrow and suffering enough to disarm all hostility.
– Henry Wadsworth Longfellow

PRAYER
Some suggestions . . .

> Dear Lord, thank You for the many
> ways You nurture me.

> Dear Lord, please help me to be more
> sensitive to the needs of others.

> Dear Lord, please help me to care
> for others and lovingly support them.

THOUGHTS & ATTITUDES
Meditate on Scriptures like these . . .

Psalm 55:22

Luke 10:33-36

Acts 24:23

I Corinthians 13

Ephesians 6:4

I Peter 5:6-7

Affirm thoughts like these . . .
- We all need help.
- How can I help the people around me?
- What do I have that someone else needs?

Other suggestions . . .
- Remember that you could be a blessing in the life of some other person.
- Remember the people whom the Lord has used to bless your life.
- Think more often of the needs of others.

Love seeks one thing only: the good of the one loved.
– Thomas Merton

WORDS

Suggested things to say or write to others . . .

- "How can I help?"
- "I'm inspired by all you do for others!"
- "You're moving on Saturday? I'll be there!"

ACTIONS

Suggestions . . .

- Give or lend things to people who need them.
- Give of your time for the benefit of others.
- Join or start a group that commits to help certain people on an ongoing basis.
- Get involved in neighborhood projects.

DISCUSSION

For personal reflection or group consideration . . .

1. What do the Scripture references in the Thoughts & Attitudes section say about nurture?

2. Why does the Lord care for us?

3. What's a good example of nurture?

4. What could I do to nurture others more?

5. What will I commit to doing?

Love is the key to the entire therapeutic program of the modern psychiatric hospital.
– Dr. Karl A. Menninger

COOPERATIVE ENHANCEMENT, TEAMWORK

**Now you are the body of Christ,
and each one of you is a part of it.**
– 1 Corinthians 12:27

Synergy is the beautiful phenomenon that occurs when people working together in harmony perform and achieve far beyond what they would accomplish separately. Synergy is combined effort that yields a combined result.

The word "synergy" is from the Greek *syn* meaning "together" and *ergon* meaning "work." Synergy is cooperatively working together. One way to think of synergy is to imagine an equation like this: $1+1=3$.

OTHER WORDS FOR SYNERGY

- concert
- conjunction
- cooperation
- teamwork

SYNERGY: IN OUR RELATIONSHIP WITH THE LORD

There's a great picture of synergy in the New Testament: the Body of Christ. Paul tells us that the Lord's followers are that body, and declares that "each one of you is a part of it." [1 Co 12:27] Paul also says that, "There are different kinds of service, but the same Lord. There are different kinds of working, but the same God works all of them in all men." [1 Co 12:5-6] Paul identifies the Lord Himself as the Head of the Body. [Col 1:18] Later Paul says that we are "created in Christ Jesus to do good works, which God prepared in advance for us to do." [Eph 2:10]

A vitally important part of the work we are called to do is to be representatives of the Lord: "We are therefore Christ's ambassadors, as though God were making His appeal through us. We implore you on Christ's behalf: Be reconciled to God. God made Him who had no sin to be sin for us, so that in Him we might become the righteousness of God. As God's fellow workers we urge you not to receive God's grace in vain." [2 Co 5:20-6:1]

We are to be fellow workers with Him and with one another, reaching out to people who need to receive His love and hear His Good News.

SYNERGY: IN OUR RELATIONSHIPS WITH OTHERS

Synergy enables people to not only work together but to accomplish more in quantity and quality than they could separately. In some cases, synergy enables people to create or achieve things that would be impossible for them to do separately.

Synergy helps fill the human need to work together to meet life's challenges. We all face things in life that are too big for us to handle alone. Synergy enables us to effectively work together to attain and achieve for the good of all.

When synergy flourishes in the Body of Christ, people are blessed. The synergy of the Spirit working together with members of the Body of Christ to the glory of God is something awesome to behold.

Symptoms and consequences . . .
HOW TO TELL WHEN SYNERGY IS WEAK OR MISSING

When synergy is weak or missing, people are not working efficiently and effectively toward shared goals. People may be more focused on achieving personal agendas than reaching team goals. They may be, as the old expression goes, "at elbows" with each other. Energy and creativity are wasted in non-productive friction and interpersonal conflicts. People withhold their respective talents and abilities that could benefit the common objective. There is often duplication of effort, while at the same time some important tasks may be left undone.

A sports team without synergy doesn't win many games. Respective strengths and weaknesses of various players are disregarded. Skills of each individual player are not used to complement the skills of other players. Some positions may be overcovered, while other positions are virtually vacant. Team members are not all on the same page in the playbook.

Possible reasons . . .
WHY PEOPLE FAIL TO PRACTICE SYNERGY

Pride and independence can keep people from working together cooperatively. Selfish pursuits can crowd out a commitment to group success. The desire to get the credit or control the situation may outweigh a commitment to the team and its goals. The ball player who won't pass the ball to another player is an example of this.

Some people don't synergize well because they don't understand or commit to shared goals and methods. A lack of effective leadership contributes to this: leaders should make sure each member clearly understands the

It is evident that many great and useful objects can be attained in this world only by cooperation.
– Thomas B. Macaulay

group's goals and is committed to working together to reach them.

The lack of synergy can also happen when any member of a relationship or a group is not personally committed to relational values like *respect* or *trust*. In fact, the absence of any of the 12 Seeds principles in a group can hinder the growth of synergy.

The good harvest that results . . .
WHEN SYNERGY GROWS

Synergy provides motivational and creative energy. People who have experienced synergy know that more gets done when synergy is present. Synergy is like a catalyst that helps people harmonize and grow together to produce desired results. With synergy, an orchestra produces beautiful music.

Synergy not only enhances and coordinates individual efforts, but it enables the people involved to attain greater results. Also, it enables them to celebrate those results together. Among the many benefits when synergy grows:

- Members of the Body of Christ work together harmoniously, and the world notices
- Teamwork improves
- People contribute their respective strengths toward common goals
- People rely upon the strengths of each other
- Productivity increases, stress decreases
- Shared experiences multiply
- Relationships blossom
- Other seeds can grow

Two people working as a team will produce more than three working as individuals.
– Charles P. McCormick

PRAYER
Some suggestions . . .

Dear Lord, thank You for creating synergy.

Dear Lord, thank You for the privilege of working together with You and with others to advance Your Kingdom.

Dear Lord, please help me to work cooperatively with others.

THOUGHTS & ATTITUDES
Meditate on Scriptures like these . . .

Proverbs 27:17

Ecclesiastes 4:9-12

Amos 3:3

Matthew 19:6

I Corinthians 12:4-31

Galatians 6:2,10

Ephesians 4:7

Philippians 2:2

Affirm thoughts like these . . .
- We get a lot done when we work together!
- Things go better when we cooperate!
- We're a great team!
- Each person on our team has great potential!

We are borne for co-operation, as are the feet, the hands, the eye-lids and the upper and lower jaws.
– Marcus Aurelius

WORDS

Suggested things to say or write to others . . .

- "I'm glad we're working together!"
- "We work well as a team!"
- "We can get this done if we work together!"
- "I'm glad you're on this team!"
- "I'll take care of that part of the job."

ACTIONS

Suggestions . . .

- Respect the strengths and weaknesses of others.
- Keep personal agendas from interfering with team goals.
- Be willing to help fill in the gaps of things others may not wish to do, or are unable to do.
- Give cooperation as a gift to others.
- Celebrate working together!

DISCUSSION

For personal reflection or group consideration . . .

1. What do the Scripture references in the Thoughts & Attitudes section say about synergy?

2. With whom should we cooperate? Why?

3. What's a good example of synergy?

4. How does synergy build the Body of Christ?

5. What could I do to cooperate more with others?

6. What will I commit to doing?

POSITIVE EXPECTATIONS

**May the God of hope fill you with all joy
and peace as you trust in Him,
so that you may overflow with hope
by the power of the Holy Spirit.**

– Romans 15:13

Hope is a wish or desire accompanied by the confident expectation of its fulfillment. Hope is to expect and desire something. The word is also used to refer to confidence or trust in someone or something.

OTHER WORDS FOR HOPE

- anticipation
- aspiration
- desire
- expectation

HOPE: IN OUR RELATIONSHIP WITH THE LORD

The Bible identifies three abiding virtues: faith, hope and love.[1 Co 13:13] And even though love is identified as the greatest of these, it's noteworthy that hope is not only one of the three, but that it's related to both love,[Ro 5:5] and also to faith.[Heb 11:1]

The hope we have in the Lord gives us confidence and boldness.[2 Co 3:12]And this confidence helps us follow

Peter's instruction to: "Always be prepared to give an answer to everyone who asks you to give the reason for the hope that you have. But do this with gentleness and respect." ¹ Pe 3:15

The importance of hope in our relationship with the Lord is further understood when we see that it is the favorable end result of much of the difficulty we face in life. Paul states: "We know that suffering produces perseverance; perseverance, character; and character, hope. And hope does not disappoint us, because God has poured out His love into our hearts by the Holy Spirit, whom He has given us." Ro 5:3-5

HOPE: IN OUR RELATIONSHIPS WITH OTHERS

Hope keeps us going, even when the way is difficult. Hope focuses us on a better future even when the present is not as we'd like it to be. Hope enables us to live with the expectation that things will get better.

Hope helps fill the need for motivation to press on. Hope lightens our present burdens with the positive expectation that things will be better in the future.

Relationships where there is hope are relationships that grow. People in such a relationship are positive and have high expectations for the future.

Symptoms and consequences . . .
HOW TO TELL WHEN HOPE IS WEAK OR MISSING

Called hopelessness, the condition of being without hope is dreadful. People are depressed and depressing, often focused only on negative things. They find it difficult or impossible to take steps toward goals or even to set goals. Motivation and energy are low. Enthusiasm is absent. People may feel that whatever they do won't make

Hope can always cope.
– P.K. Thomajan

any difference anyway. They see no way out. Relationships are listless or non-existent. People are tempted to give up. Some do.

Possible reasons . . .
WHY PEOPLE FAIL TO HOPE

Perhaps the major reason people fail to hope, and to share hope with others, is that they do not rest in a strong secure trust in the Lord. They fail to respect His mighty ability to nurture them in the future, and they fail to trust that He actually will. They forget the Lord's many promises to bless them.

Young people at times will fail to hope because they lack the life experiences that teach us that, even though we may be in a valley now, we may be walking on higher ground soon.

Other people are so exhausted from the trials and challenges they've been through that they can't see any way that the future will be any different. They may be neglecting rest and relaxation. They may not be getting the "re-creation" they need.

And of course there are the people who borrow trouble from the future – called worrying – and become overwhelmed by obstacles and problems that seem so much bigger than any strength or resources they have today. Some of these people look only to their own strengths and resources: they fail to see the great resources of the Lord. They forget that He can make available resources now or in the future – often through other people.

Then there are people who have no defined purpose or goals in life. They feel they aren't making any headway in life – they miss the hope-giving effect of seeing progress made toward worthy objectives.

Whatever enlarges hope will also exalt courage.
– Samuel Johnson

There are others who grew up in environments where hopelessness and pessimism ruled, where there may have been the tendency to dwell on bad news – both actual bad news and also possible bad news. Even good news may have been tempered with a negative slant. Some people still live in such environments.

People who fail to hope forget that they have a choice: they can focus on the problem(s), or they can focus on the Lord. They can choose to focus on the negative, or they can choose the positive.

The good harvest that results . . .
WHEN HOPE GROWS

When hope grows, everything looks better and feels better. People are motivated, inspired, and willing to work through present difficulties with the expectation that the future will bring a better situation or a greater achievement. A few benefits when hope grows:
- The Lord is honored as His people hope in Him
- People outside the Body of Christ notice
- Energy and enthusiasm are revitalized
- Hope is contagious and positively affects others
- People maintain a vision of better things even though the present may be difficult
- People focus on the more important things in life
- Relationships grow

Ah, Hope! What would life be, stripped of thy encouraging smiles, that teach us to look behind the dark clouds of today, for the golden beams that are to gild the morrow.
– Susanna Moodie

PRAYER

Some suggestions . . .

> Dear Lord, thank You for the hope I have in You.
>
> Dear Lord, please help me to radiate
> Your hope to others.
>
> Dear Lord, please help me to brighten
> every room I walk into.

THOUGHTS & ATTITUDES

Meditate on Scriptures like these . . .

> Isaiah 40:31
>
> Isaiah 49:23
>
> Jeremiah 29:11
>
> Lamentations 3:24-26
>
> Romans 12:12
>
> Romans 15:4,13
>
> Hebrews 6:11, 18-19a

Affirm thoughts like these . . .

- With the Lord's help, I know we can make it.
- We'll get through.
- It's going to be wonderful!

Other suggestions . . .

- Focus on the Lord, rather than on the problem.
- Meditate on the Lord's promises.
- Remember that the Lord has brought you through many challenges in the past.

Waitings which ripen hopes are not delays.
– Edward Benlowes

WORDS

Suggested things to say or write to others . . .

- "We're making progress!"
- "It will be worth it!"
- "Better things are coming!"

Other suggestions . . .

- Avoid spreading gossip or rumors.
- Avoid negative remarks.

ACTIONS

Suggestions . . .

- Share hope with others: give hope as a gift.
- Get the rest you need.
- Smile.
- Sing.

DISCUSSION

For personal reflection or group consideration . . .

1. What do the Scripture references in the Thoughts & Attitudes section say about hope?

2. Where is the source of our hope?

3. What's a good example of hope?

4. How well do I radiate hope? Explain.

5. Do I know someone who lacks hope? If so, what can I do to help that person gain hope?

6. What could I do to help give more hope to others?

7. What will I commit to doing?

IDEALS

VALUES AND MODELS OF EXCELLENCE

**Whatever is true, whatever is noble,
whatever is right, whatever is pure,
whatever is lovely, whatever is admirable –
if anything is excellent or praiseworthy –
think about such things.**

– Philippians 4:8

Ideals are the high standards and examples that are worthy of imitation and replication in a life of excellence. Ideals are the high patterns and models that guide quality living.

Ideals are in many forms, such as beautiful scenery that inspires us, goals that guide us, examples that motivate us, worthy principles that help orient our lives. Each of the 12 Seeds, for example, is a practical ideal for living.

Our highest ideal, of course, is our Lord Himself.

OTHER WORDS FOR IDEALS

- examples
- models
- principles
- standards
- virtues

IDEALS: IN OUR RELATIONSHIP WITH THE LORD

To be in relationship with the Lord is to know the One who is the epitome of excellence and high ideals. His standards and His ways are perfect. His righteousness is complete. As we grow closer to Him, our thoughts, words and actions become, with His help and by His power, more and more like His.

The Lord has sent His Spirit to live inside us and remind us of His truth.[Jn 14:26] He helps us think about excellent things,[Php 4:8] and do excellent works.[Titus 3:8] And, He produces excellent fruit in our lives: "love, joy, peace, patience, kindness, goodness, faithfulness, gentleness and self-control."[Gal 5:22-23] Each part of that fruit is an ideal that blesses people and enhances relationships.

Though we live now in a world where many things are less than ideal, someday He will take us into the ideal place He has prepared for us. For now, we can dwell upon the beauty and joy of knowing Him and following Him in our lives.[Col 2:9-10]

IDEALS: IN OUR RELATIONSHIPS WITH OTHERS

Our Lord created us to live and work together with Him and with others in the beautiful Garden of Eden. Someday He will take us to an even more perfect place, as mentioned above. When ideals are part of our relationships, we can remind one another of these and other uplifting truths. And in so doing we help fulfill our need to focus on things higher than ourselves.

Our Lord created us to enjoy living and working in harmony with Him and with one another. As we relate to Him and to one another, we can pray that His ideals would permeate our prayers, thoughts, words, actions and discussions. We can share a "bit of heaven" with one another. We can talk and sing of His love, His Creation, His beauty and His grace. We can celebrate the changes we see Him bringing about in each other's lives. We can celebrate the higher quality of living He provides as we live and work in communion together.

Symptoms and consequences . . .
HOW TO TELL WHEN IDEALS ARE WEAK OR MISSING

Without ideals, life can be like traveling through beautiful country and missing the scenery because we're preoccupied with the dirt on the car window.

When ideals are missing in a relationship, thoughts are often evil and self-appeasing. Communication is typically centered on trivial topics and peppered with profanity. Animal instincts drive much activity. Behavioral standards are pushed ever lower. Respect for truth and character is absent. Inspiration to pursue higher things is absent. Daily life can range from a dull emptiness to an aggressive pursuit of evil.

Relationships without ideals are unfulfilling, lifeless, uninspiring, unrewarding, misguided, dull.

Possible reasons . . .
WHY PEOPLE FAIL TO UPHOLD IDEALS

Looking away from the Lord is perhaps the primary reason people fail to uphold high ideals. When Peter took his eyes off the Lord and instead looked at the swirling waves, he began to sink.[Mt 14:28-30] That happens to us too whenever we fail to focus on the Lord.

Some people never learned about ideals. They may have grown up in environments where ideals were ignored and where all the attention was given to base things – where the profane received all the attention and the profound was ridiculed. Some people still live or work in such environments, rarely if ever seeing a good human role model for the practice of ideals.

Other people fail to uphold high ideals – such as a goal or performance standard, because at one time they tried and failed to do so. They may have become discouraged and quit. Still other people are simply lazy and don't want the discipline of pursuing ideals.

It can be easy to fail to uphold ideals in society today, where good is often called bad and bad is often called good. Without a focus on the Lord, it's easy to settle for values and models that are far less than His high ideals.

The good harvest that results . . .
WHEN IDEALS GROW

Ideals lift our spirits, calling us to higher things. They give higher meaning and purpose to our lives together. Ideals give us direction. They give us high goals toward which to shoot. Ideals inspire us, providing beauty for our lives. They remind us of the excellence of our Lord and His handiwork.

As we focus on ideals together, we lift our lives and our relationships from the profane to the profound. When ideals are upheld, we reap many blessings:
- We focus more on the Lord and His ways
- People are inspired toward noble pursuits
- High standards of conduct are maintained
- People focus more on the important things in life
- Thoughts are not captivated and held down by the lower things in life
- Inspiration and creativity increase
- Quality of life improves

> **He who, having lost one ideal, refuses to give his heart and soul to another and nobler, is like a man who declines to build a house on the rock because the wind and rain have ruined his house on the sand.**
> – Constance Naden

PRAYER
Some suggestions . . .

> Dear Lord, thank You for revealing some of Your excellence and majesty to me.
>
> Dear Lord, help me to focus on You and on the high values You wish me to live by.
>
> Dear Lord, help me to add your high values and patterns of excellence to my relationships.

THOUGHTS & ATTITUDES
Meditate on Scriptures like these . . .

> Psalm 8
>
> Psalm 19
>
> Psalm 34:1
>
> Philippians 3:17
>
> Philippians 4:8-9
>
> Colossians 3:12-17
>
> 1 Peter 1:7

Affirm thoughts like these . . .
- The heavens declare the glory of God!
- There is so much beauty in the world!
- People are amazingly complex and wonderful!
- I will strive for excellence!

Other suggestions . . .
- Meditate on Scripture, such as the Psalms.
- Memorize Scripture.
- Replace profane and negative thoughts with profound and positive thoughts.
- Dwell on the Lord and His ways.

WORDS

Suggested things to say or write to others . . .

- "Look at what this passage of Scripture says: (share a Psalm or other Bible passage)."
- "I admire your high values."
- "You have a refined sense of beauty."
- "I'm inspired by your high standards."
- "What's the best way to do this?"
- "What would Jesus do in this situation?"

ACTIONS

Suggestions . . .

- Worship the Lord throughout the day.
- Avoid profanity.
- Be careful about your choices of media.
- Look into the starry heavens at night.
- Look upon great art, listen to inspiring music.
- Share uplifting ideas, dreams, goals.
- Develop and follow a vision or mission statement

DISCUSSION

For personal reflection or group consideration . . .

1. What do the Scripture references in the Thoughts & Attitudes section say about ideals?

2. What's a good example of an ideal being upheld?

3. What could I do to inspire higher ideals in others?

4. What will I commit to doing?

To live in the presence of great truths and eternal laws, to be led by permanent ideals – that is what keeps a person patient when the world ignores him, and calm and unspoiled when the world praises him.

– Honore de Balzac

FORGIVENESS AND RELEASE

**Bear with each other and forgive whatever
grievances you may have against one another.
Forgive as the Lord forgave you.**

– Colossians 3:13

Pardon is forgiveness of an offense or cancellation of a penalty. It involves excusing someone for what they did or for what they failed to do. Pardon provides the offender with release from penalty; it provides the one granting pardon with release from bitterness. In effect, pardon is "letting go."

OTHER WORDS FOR PARDON

- absolution
- amnesty
- forgiveness
- release

PARDON: IN OUR RELATIONSHIP WITH THE LORD

When we think of how pardon is involved in our relationship with the Lord, overwhelming gratitude should fill our hearts! In fact, gratitude for His pardon should be one of the primary ways we practice the seed of Appreciation. It is only when we begin to realize how holy and righteous the Lord is, and how unholy and unrighteous we are apart from Him, that we even start to appreciate how valuable His pardon is to us.

If it were not for pardon, unholy rebellious creatures like us could not have any relationship with a holy, perfect God. The Bible makes it very clear that all of us have sinned against God. [Ro 3:23] But the Good News, the Gospel, is that when we turn to the Lord, "He will freely pardon." [Is 55:7] Pardon makes it possible for us to have an ongoing, growing relationship with Him!

Pardon in our relationship with the Lord is in a sense only one-way between the Lord and us. He pardons us, but since He is perfect, there is nothing for which we can in turn forgive Him. However, we can respond with thanksgiving and obedience. We obey him when we in turn forgive others, as we shall see in the next section.

PARDON: IN OUR RELATIONSHIPS WITH OTHERS

Jesus taught that since we've been forgiven, we should forgive others. He said, "For if you forgive men when they sin against you, your heavenly Father will also forgive you. But if you do not forgive men their sins, your Father will not forgive your sins." [Mt 6:14-15]

In His parable about the "Unmerciful Servant" Jesus told of a servant who was forgiven an enormous debt by his master. Yet, this servant was unmerciful and would not forgive a much smaller debt owed to him by a fellow servant. The master was angry with the servant and severely punished him. [Mt 18:23-35]

Forgiving others is an act of obedience and also an expression of gratitude to the Lord for the pardon He has granted us. It can also be a way that we can get the attention of people so that they'll listen to the Good News of the Lord's willingness to pardon them.

Good to forget – Best to forgive!
– Robert Browning

Symptoms and consequences . . .
HOW TO TELL WHEN PARDON IS WEAK OR MISSING

When pardon is lacking, people hold grudges that sometimes grow far out of all proportion to the offense. The drive for revenge may become intense. Relationships can be poisoned. Mental energy can be wasted trying to understand why someone said or did something. The person who offended is not granted freedom to go on and to grow; the person withholding pardon is in bondage to resentment and bitterness. It is a very unhappy way to live. And it adversely affects not only the people involved, but also the people around them.

Possible reasons . . .
WHY PEOPLE FAIL TO PARDON

People who fail to pardon may never have experienced or witnessed it in their own lives. Some grew up in families where grudges were held for years. Others still live or work in such environments.

Some people may think that if they forgive they will only encourage the forgiven one to commit the offense again. They'd rather cling to bitterness and keep the other person saddled with continuing guilt.

Other people may want to emphasize – to others and to themselves – how greatly they were injured. They think that not forgiving is a way to punish the offender. They don't realize that in failing to forgive they may be hurting themselves more than the other person. As someone once said, "Failing to forgive someone is like drinking poison and expecting the other person to get sick."

Perhaps the major reason people fail to pardon others is that they have either failed to ask for and receive the Lord's pardon in their own lives – or, having received that great pardon, they neglect to obey the Lord's command to in turn forgive others.

The good harvest that results . . .
WHEN PARDON GROWS

Pardon does so much for interpersonal relationships! It releases people to go forward. It acknowledges that we all do things that harm other people, sometimes greatly. And yet we can forgive and move on.

Pardon frees us from bitterness and resentment. It removes the drive for revenge, and even the need to completely understand why an offense was committed.

Pardon helps fill the human need for forgiveness, so that people are free to move on and grow together. We all want relationships that are strong enough to endure mistakes and transgressions. When pardon is present, it means that the commitment to one another surpasses any irritations and offenses. A summary of some of the benefits when pardon is present:

- Relationships continue to develop
- People receive the blessing of forgiveness
- Reconciliation, if needed, is possible
- People around the parties involved also benefit
- Stress decreases
- Others see how pardon works, and may start practicing it in their relationships
- People focus less on the minor irritations of life
- People invest more time and energy in the more important things in life
- Some people, who may never before have asked for the Lord's pardon, may seek it

To err is human, to forgive divine.
– Alexander Pope

PRAYER

Some suggestions . . .

> Dear Lord, thank You for the pardon You have mercifully and graciously given me.

> Dear Lord, please help me to tell others the Good News that You offer them pardon.

> Dear Lord, please help me to graciously pardon those who commit offenses against me.

THOUGHTS & ATTITUDES

Meditate on Scriptures like these . . .

> Exodus 34:9
>
> Nehemiah 9:17
>
> Psalm 51:1-3
>
> Matthew 6:12-15
>
> Matthew 18:21-22
>
> Colossians 3:13

Affirm thoughts like these . . .

- The Lord has forgiven me of so much!
- I appreciate that others have pardoned me.
- With the Lord's help, I can forgive _____.
- Pardon renews relationships.
- Pardon releases us to move on together.

A wise man will make haste to forgive, because he knows the true value of time, and will not suffer it to pass away in unnecessary pain.

– Samuel Johnson

WORDS

Suggested things to say or write to others . . .

- "Pardon me."
- "I'm sorry for what I did."
- "Please forgive me."
- "I forgive you. Let's go forward together!"

ACTIONS

Suggestions . . .

- Pray the words from the Lord's Prayer: "Forgive us our debts, as we forgive our debtors."
- Thank the Lord for the pardon He has provided.
- Let go of grudges.
- Write a letter asking for forgiveness.
- Write a letter granting forgiveness.

DISCUSSION

For personal reflection or group consideration . . .

1. What do the Scripture references in the Thoughts & Attitudes section say about pardon?

2. What's a good example of pardon?

3. How does pardon build the Body of Christ?

4. How could I be more forgiving toward others?

5. What will I commit to doing?

There is nothing so advantageous to a man as a forgiving disposition.

– Terence

Forgiveness is the fragrance the violet sheds on the heel that has crushed it.

– Samuel Clemens

The 12 Seeds RELATIONSHIP Acrostic

The 12 Seeds RELATIONSHIP acrostic shown here is a handy way to remember all twelve relationship building principles.

An acrostic is a series of words or phrases arranged so the first letters form a word or other pattern. Acrostics have long been used to remember important concepts. Psalms 9 and 10, for example, are called Acrostic Psalms since each verse begins with the succeeding letter of the Hebrew alphabet.

12 Seeds™

RESPECT
ENCOURAGEMENT
LISTENING
APPRECIATION
TRUST
INTEGRITY
ORDER
NURTURE
SYNERGY
HOPE
IDEALS
PARDON

PRAYER
THOUGHTS
WORDS
ACTIONS
DISCUSSION

©2004 12 Seeds International, Inc.

In addition to helping you remember all twelve principles, this acrostic can also serve as a checklist for qualities to promote in your family, team, group, church, business or community.

We've placed the "Five Habits" in the bottom right corner of the diagram above, to remind you of the five different types of practical applications presented in each "seed chapter." These five habits are discussed in greater detail in Part II.

" . . . seed fell on good soil, where it produced a crop – a hundred, sixty or thirty times what was sown."

From the Parable of the Sower, Matthew 13:8 NIV

RESPECT
ENCOURAGEMENT
LISTENING
APPRECIATION
TRUST
INTEGRITY
ORDER
NURTURE
SYNERGY
HOPE
IDEALS
PARDON

PART II

Plant and Cultivate!

Growing Successful Relationships

What Everyone Should Know about Seeds

A seed is "the source, origin or beginning of anything." Therefore, we sometimes say things like the "seeds of a new era," the "seeds of invention," the "seeds of revival." In plants, a seed is the part of the plant that contains the embryo, which is an early or undeveloped stage of the plant.

SEEDS ARE INFLUENCES!

Seeds are also influences. Each of the 12 Seeds is an influence that helps relationships grow. Each seed is a positive influence upon individuals and upon the cultural environment. The potential impact is great.

The word *influence* can be defined as "in-flowance" to the mind. When you speak words of respect, encouragement, appreciation and hope to others, people may be hearing positive things they seldom hear. And when your actions include such things as listening, nurture and integrity, people may be experiencing positive things they seldom see. It *will* make an impact upon them, and they in turn are much more likely to treat others in a better way. The influence can multiply.

> **"The word *influence* can be defined as 'in-flowance' to the mind."**

Unfortunately, some "inflowances" are negative and destructive, tending to tear down people and relationships rather than building them up. We need more positive "in-flowances." When you think about the principles of the 12 Seeds, and how to apply them in your life, you're cultivating positive influences in your mind.

Furthermore, when you practice the principles in your relationships, your words and actions are like seeds that are being planted in the lives of other people. As you plant and cultivate the seeds, keep in mind that:

Seeds are . . .
- small yet powerful
- tough and durable
- valuable
- humble – they get dirt thrown on them – yet, *seeds grow in the dirt*
- the product of successful growth
- a vital part of new growth
- sometimes carried by the wind or by creatures
- mentioned often in the Bible: 256 times in the KJV; 80 times in the NIV
- mentioned in several parables Jesus told
- mentioned at the beginning of the Bible [Ge 1:11]
- mentioned toward the end of the Bible [1 Jn 3:9]

Seeds also . . .
- travel widely
- take time to sprout and grow
- have great potential, at times yielding a harvest of 30, 60, or even 100 fold [Mt 13:8]

BAD SEEDS VS. GOOD SEEDS

Negative values like *disrespect* and *ingratitude* are like bad seeds that produce weeds that choke and destroy. When such weeds invade thoughts, they produce negative words and actions that hinder or block the growth of relationships.

Positive values like *respect* and *appreciation,* on the other hand, are high-quality, high-potential seeds. When planted and cultivated in the mind, they produce positive words and actions that enhance relationships and overall quality of life.

The chart on the next page shows the "bad seeds" and the "good seeds" summarized from the seed chapters in Part I. The chart can be helpful in determining if any "bad seeds" are present in your relationships or in your environment. Look to the right side of the chart for the corresponding "good seeds" that are needed.

THE LAW OF SOWING AND REAPING, WITH COROLLARIES

There's a principle related to seeds that's known as the Law of Sowing and Reaping. It is: "You reap what you sow." It's based upon Paul's admonition to the people in Galatia: "Do

> THE LAW OF SOWING AND REAPING
> **"You reap what you sow."**

not be deceived. God cannot be mocked. A man reaps what he sows." [Ga 6:7] The Law has several corollaries:

1. You reap more than you sow.
2. You reap later than you sow.
3. You reap of the same kind as you sow.

Two more facts that are good to remember: 1. The law applies to both good seeds and bad seeds; and 2. The Lord has promised to provide for and bless those who sow good seeds. Consider this verse:

> **Remember this: Whoever sows sparingly will also reap sparingly, and whoever sows generously will also reap generously . . . Now He who supplies seed to the sower and bread for food will also supply and increase your store of seed and will enlarge the harvest of your righteousness.**
> – II Corinthians 9:6,10

INFLUENCES THAT AFFECT RELATIONSHIPS

BAD SEEDS vs. GOOD SEEDS   12 Seeds™
negative, destructive   POSITIVE, CONSTRUCTIVE

disrespect	**RESPECT**
rudeness	REGARD, ESTEEM, HONOR
discouragement	**ENCOURAGEMENT**
negativity	INSPIRING WITH COURAGE
inattentiveness	**LISTENING**
insensitivity	STRIVING TO HEAR; HEEDING
ingratitude	**APPRECIATION**
unappreciativeness	GRATEFUL RECOGNITION OF VALUE
distrust	**TRUST**
suspicion	CONFIDENCE IN ANOTHER
dishonesty	**INTEGRITY**
infidelity	MORAL STRENGTH & WHOLENESS
disorder	**ORDER**
confusion	STRUCTURE, PRIORITIES, GUIDELINES
self-centeredness	**NURTURE**
uncaring spirit	CARE & FEEDING, LOVING SUPPORT
uncooperativeness	**SYNERGY**
discord	COOPERATION, TEAMWORK
hopelessness	**HOPE**
pessimism	POSITIVE EXPECTATIONS
baseness	**IDEALS**
profanity	VALUES AND MODELS OF EXCELLENCE
unforgiveness	**PARDON**
resentment	FORGIVENESS AND RELEASE

THE HARVEST
A thorny weedpatch vs. **A BEAUTIFUL GARDEN**

THE GOOD SEEDS HELP FILL NEEDS

Each seed chapter makes reference to a need that the seed helps fill. As you plant and cultivate a seed, you're giving a gift that can help fill a human need. It's part of the harvest resulting from growing the seeds. The needs that the seeds help fill are summarized on page 113 in the chapter entitled: "Anticipate the Harvest."

KEEP PLANTING AND CULTIVATING

It's important to keep planting and cultivating positive influences. Here are a few of the reasons:

1. **Negative influences abound.** Therefore, we need to make positive influences abundant.

2. **Repetition reinforces importance.**

3. **Repetition helps us learn.**

4. **We forget.** Even after learning, we need reminders. Remember Samuel Johnson's statement, as quoted by C. S. Lewis: "People need to be reminded more often than they need to be instructed."

5. **Repetition helps make the principles part of our thinking,** so that the principles become part of our lives!

BE A POSITIVE INFLUENCE!

Plant and cultivate the seeds!

ONE WAY TO BE A POSITIVE INFLUENCE:

After you've read through this book for the first time, invite someone you care about – or a group – to go through it with you. Discuss and grow together.

YOU'LL BENEFIT EVEN MORE + THEY'LL BENEFIT + YOUR RELATIONSHIPS WILL GROW!

Five Habits for Success

There are five types of activities that can be thought of as groups of habits that help build successful relationships: Prayer, Thoughts & Attitudes, Words, Actions and Discussion. The "Practical Applications" section of each "seed chapter" in Part I of this book presents examples of each of these habits.

A habit is defined as "a recurrent, often unconscious pattern of behavior that's acquired through frequent repetition." It's a customary manner or way of doing things. A habit is part of our *practice* – the way we conduct our lives. Our principles are also part of our practice. A principle is a rule or standard of good behavior. Prin-

> **"Principles should guide habits."**

ciples should guide habits. The 12 Seeds are twelve principles that can be used with the five types of habits mentioned here.

1. PRAYER

Prayer is communion and communication with the Lord. We can define "communion" as fellowship or sharing. The word is based upon the Latin *communio,* meaning "mutual participation" and *communis,* meaning "common." "Communication" is based upon the same Latin words, and refers to the transmission of thoughts, messages or information.

Some people use the ACTS acrostic as a structure for

their prayers. ACTS stands for: Adoration, Confession, Thanksgiving, and Supplication (Petition).

Applying the ACTS acrostic to relationships, we can include in our prayers: (A) Adoration: praise the Lord for His greatness; (C) Confession: admit that we don't always relate to Him and to others in loving ways; (T) Thanksgiving: thank Him for our relationship with Him, and with others; and (S) Supplication: ask Him to help us grow in all our relationships.

Someone once said that we should "talk to God about people before we talk to people about God." This is good advice to follow whenever we're seeking to help someone grow in their relationship with the Lord, or in their relationships with other people.

It's very likely that you'll find, as you study the seeds, that you're becoming better able to discern when people are not practicing all twelve principles very well (and this may include you). Our natural human tendency is to be critical of them instead of praying for them. Oswald Chambers refers to this and to the importance of intercessory prayer when he says, "Discernment is God's call to intercession, never to fault finding."

> **"Discernment is God's call to intercession, never to fault-finding."**
> – Oswald Chambers

As you study the 12 Seeds and learn to better identify when a seed is weak or missing, use the discernment you gain as a call to prayer rather than criticism.

2. THOUGHTS & ATTITUDES

The Bible has a lot to say about thoughts and attitudes, and it gives us this description of man: "as he thinketh in his heart, so is he." [Pr 23:7 KJV] Remember that the Bible uses the words "heart" and "mind" to refer to what's inside a person, the person's essence. In this book we use the words *thoughts* and *attitudes* to refer to the activities of our minds, including our holding of beliefs and values, as well as our intentions and perceptions. These are things that are inside us.

In simple terms, *thoughts* are *what* we think about, and *attitudes* are *how we feel* about what we think about. Our attitudes are the perceptions and emotions we have about things, the particular "slant on things" that we hold. Someone has said that an attitude is like the "angle of approach" of an airplane.

We use the word *meditation* to refer to the intentional practice of focusing upon a particular subject, such as a passage of Scripture. This focus can also be called "priming" the mind. In each "seed chapter" there are Scripture passages as well as other suggestions to help you prime your mind about the seed.

What we seek, of course, are more *good* thoughts and *good* attitudes. Those are the thoughts and attitudes that yield good words and good actions. What happens in our minds precedes what happens in our words and in our actions. That's why it's wise to prime your mind often with positive principles like the 12 Seeds, to guide words and actions so they will help produce a harvest of desirable results.

> **"What happens in our minds precedes what happens in our words and in our actions."**

Do not conform any longer to the pattern
of this world, but be transformed by the
renewing of your mind. Then you will be able
to test and approve what God's will is –
His good, pleasing and perfect will.
– Romans 12:2

3. WORDS

Our words reveal what is inside us, in our thoughts and attitudes. If love is inside us, we will speak loving words to others. If respect is a value we hold, we will speak respectfully to others. Our words are expressions of the principles that guide our lives.

Words are of course an important element of communication. Communication is absolutely essential in any relationship, and can be defined as: "transmission of thoughts, messages or information by speech, signals, writing or behavior."

> **"Our words are expressions of the principles that guide our lives."**

Remember that the word "communication" is based upon the Latin word for "common." Therefore, we could think of communication as the activity by which we arrive at a common understanding of thoughts, messages or information.

Words are powerful. The old saying, "Sticks and stones may break my bones, but words will never hurt me" is not true. Someone has restated this in a more accurate way: "Sticks and stones may break my bones, but words will break my heart."

Words can harm or break a relationship quickly. More often, harmful words slowly chip away, tearing down people and tearing down relationships.

On the other hand, words can be powerful tools for healing, and for blessing other people. They can be essential in building, restoring and maintaining relationships. They can actually be *benedictions* we share with one another frequently in daily life.

The Bible has a lot to say about our mouths,
our lips, our tongues, for our speech betrays us.
What is down in the well will come up in the bucket.
– Vance Havner

We usually think of a benediction as the blessing given at the end of a worship service. Yet, such a blessing does not need to be limited to a time and place. The word benediction comes from the Latin *bene,* meaning good, and *diction,* meaning words. A benediction is really: *good words.* In a world filled with so many negative, harmful words, we need more benedictions!

> **"A benediction
> is really:
> good words."**

Good words are a joy to give and to receive. Just imagine what they could do for people and for relationships! Let's develop vocabularies with more benedictions!

> **May the words of my mouth and the meditation
> of my heart be pleasing in Your sight,
> O LORD, my Rock and my Redeemer.**
>
> – Psalm 19:14

4. ACTIONS

Our actions are demonstrations of the principles that guide our lives. Our actions reveal our beliefs and values. This relationship between what's inside us and our behavior is pointed out by the apostle James when he says: "I will show you my faith by what I do." [Ja 2:18]

After a person does something that's hard to explain, we're sometimes reminded of the link between what we think and what we do. People may ask, "What was she thinking?" Or, "What got into his head?" On the other hand, when someone does a good deed – a good *action* – for another person, we hear people say things like "Oh, how *thoughtful!*"

> **All that a person does outwardly is but the
> expression and completion of his inward thought.
> To work effectually, he must think clearly;
> to act nobly, he must think nobly.**
>
> – Channing

People notice if our actions align with our words. They see if we "practice what we preach." You may recognize this quote from the seed chapter on *Integrity*: "People may doubt what you say, but they will always believe what you do." If we want good actions

> **"Our actions are demonstrations of the principles that guide our lives."**

in our lives, we must focus on planting and cultivating good principles in our thoughts and attitudes. Therefore, before trying to practice the suggested "Actions" in each seed chapter, meditate on the suggested "Thoughts & Attitudes."

Good actions bring benefits. It's interesting that the word "benefit" is from the Old French *bienfait,* meaning "good deed" and from the Latin words *benefactum* and *benefacere,* meaning "to do a service."

5. DISCUSSION

Discussion is the consideration of a subject by a group. It includes conversation and examination of a topic by two or more people.

One of the pleasant discoveries, after the release of the first edition of this book, was the many engaging discussions it prompted. It's as if the 12 Seeds come alive in discussion. A teacher friend describes this phenomenon with the phrase, "the discovery is in the discussion."

It's in good discussion that we have those "Ah ha!" experiences where certain things become more clear to us. It's in discussion that we benefit from the synergy of various thoughts and ideas. The many benefits of good communication can be experienced together in discussion, as we share specific insights or applications with one another. Often one person's willingness to tell a personal insight or experience will open up an important understanding in the mind of someone else.

Discussion can be very relational and communal. A 12 Seeds discussion, for example, is an opportunity to not only learn more about the principles and habits of relationship-building, but can also be a time in which we actually practice all twelve principles and all five habits in fellowship with one another. In a sense, such discussion can be a form of communion among

> ". . . discussion can be a form of communion among people."

people. Remember, communion means "common participation."

Our discussion times can actually include practicing the 12 Seeds. For example, we can have respectful communication with the Lord, and with one another. We can encourage one another, listen to one another, appreciate what others say, and so on. The seeds can blossom during our discussion experiences.

12 Seeds discussions can be wonderful times for individual growth and for building up the Body of Christ. Suggestions for discussing the seeds in a class or group are included in the back of this book.

We urge you to discuss the 12 Seeds with others.

How to Overcome the Weeds

Overcoming the forces that harm relationships

There are a number of forces that work against the development and growth of good relationships. These forces are like weeds that can choke out the growth of the seeds. Some of these forces are mentioned in the seed chapters in Part I of this book.

It's good to be able to recognize when these weeds are adversely affecting relationships. It's even better to take steps to overcome them.

SOME WEEDS THAT HARM RELATIONSHIPS

1. Failure to follow our Lord's example
2. Pride and self-centeredness
3. Apathy about relationships
4. A "nice to know" attitude about the seeds
5. Lack of training and discipline
6. Distractions and forgetfulness
7. The myth that people can't change
8. Bad influences or "bad seeds"
9. Enemy activity

SUGGESTED WAYS TO OVERCOME THE WEEDS:

To overcome the failure to follow our Lord's example . . .

1. Keep your eyes on the Lord. Notice how He cares for and loves people. Avoid initiatives and responses that are based upon how the world treats people. Instead, watch the Lord. Consider Him to be your perfect model for relationship-building. Ask Him for help with all relationships.

To overcome pride and self-centeredness . . .

2. Be more other-centered rather than self-centered. Give respect, encouragement and the other seeds as gifts to people around you. Think more highly, and more often, of others. Be a blessing to them.

To overcome apathy about relationships . . .

3. Remember the importance and the benefits of good relationships. Realize that urgent things often crowd out truly important things in life. Be aware that many of the urgent "fires" that consume our time and energy are in fact caused by poor relationships. Remember the life-changing benefits of good relationships in every area of life.

To overcome a "nice to know" attitude about the seeds . . .

4. Adopt a motivational attitude toward the seeds. If you think of the 12 Seeds as principles that are just "nice to know," then it's very likely that you'll do very little to plant and cultivate them in your life. However, if you adopt a "motivational attitude" toward them, you're more likely to make them part of your life. For example, when you think of the seeds as "Ways to Love," or "Marriage & Family Values," or "Agents of Change," then you're much more likely to practice them regularly and reap their benefits in your life. The next chapter offers more help on this.

To overcome lack of training and discipline . . .

5. **Learn, and encourage others to learn,** the basic principles of good relationships. Become intentional about making the principles part of your daily habits. Also, remember that some people never learned principles like the 12 Seeds, or how to practice all twelve in daily life. Don't be angry or impatient with such folks. Instead, pray for them. Help them learn the basics of good relationships. Be a good role model for them. Encourage mutual accountability in your relationships with them.

> **Study to show thyself approved unto God . . .**
> **rightly dividing the word of truth.**
> – 2 Timothy 2:15

To overcome distractions and forgetfulness . . .

6. **Remind self and others about the 12 Seeds** on an ongoing basis. The many distractions of life can cause us to forget to apply what we know. We need to remind ourselves often of the principles and habits that yield good relationships.

> **People need to be reminded more often**
> **than they need to be instructed.**
> – Samuel Johnson, as quoted by C.S. Lewis

To overcome the myth that people can't change . . .

7. **Understand that people do change.** At times we give up on people and relationships, thinking they'll never change. But they do. Consider:

> **Some pessimists would say that no one**
> **changes, that the leopard never changes**
> **his spots. But in fact everyone is**
> **changing every day, either for better**
> **or for worse . . . *Of course* they change,**
> **and we can influence, to some extent**
> **at least, how they change.**
> – Alan Loy McGinnis

To overcome bad influences or "bad seeds" . . .

8. Continue to plant and cultivate good seeds. The "bad seeds" are the negative influences and practices that work against relationships. To help recognize them, see the "Bad Seeds vs. Good Seeds" comparison chart on page 93. Remember that negative influences abound. We need to make positive influences abundant. When we encounter the bad seeds, we may be tempted to respond in kind. For example, when someone shows disrespect toward us, the temptation is to disrespect them in return. Instead, continue to plant good seeds.

> **Do not be overcome by evil,**
> **but overcome evil with good.**
> – Romans 12:21

To overcome enemy activity . . .

9. Pray. Be aware that Satan seeks to destroy relationships. He hates to see strong families, lasting friendships and loving communities. Though we ourselves may at times promote or allow the march of the forces mentioned above, we should remember that Satan will do whatever he can to further help those forces advance against relationships. The enemy loves to see the weeds infiltrating our thoughts, words, actions and discussions. We need to pray for discernment to recognize when those forces are present. We need to pray for wisdom and help in overcoming the weeds.

> **Pray continually.**
> – 1 Thessalonians 5:17

Get Motivated!

Motivational attitudes toward the 12 Seeds

You can think of the 12 Seeds as things that are "nice to know," as mentioned in the last chapter. Or, you can look at the seeds as transformational ingredients for a rich and rewarding life. Your attitude toward the 12 Seeds will determine if, and how, you make them part of your life. Consider the following ways to think of the seeds, then choose one or a few of the ways that will motivate you to plant and cultivate them on a daily basis. Here are some of the possible ways to think of the seeds:

> "Your attitude toward the 12 Seeds will determine if, and how, you make them part of your life."

Ways to Love
Marriage & Family Values
Body Builders
Gifts that Fill Needs
Learning for a Lifetime
Agents of Change
Steps Toward Reconciliation
Seeds of General Goodwill
Seeds of Business Goodwill
Core Values

WAYS TO LOVE

Our Lord makes it clear that love is to be an essential part of our life together as members of His Body. Our relationships are to be characterized by loving ways that honor His commands and bless one another. He said that love for one another will be a distinguishing

"A new command I give you: Love one another."
– John 13:34

mark that will tell others that we follow Him. Our love is to be a powerful witness to the world.

Just how do we love others in practical terms? If love is "seeking the highest welfare of the one loved," just how do we do that? The 12 Seeds are twelve of the ways we can do that. Planting and cultivating the seeds can be habitual yet refreshing ways to love others. People will be blessed as we obey our Lord's command to love.

MARRIAGE & FAMILY VALUES

A family is where the basic principles of rich, life-long relationships should be learned, practiced and enjoyed. Solid principles should guide a family's own "best practices." The 12 Seeds can be distinguishing characteristics of a family's culture and part of its legacy. They can help each member to develop and maintain lasting relationships all through life.

BODY BUILDERS

The seeds are also ways to build up the Body of Christ. There are many corrosive attitudes, words and actions that work to tear down the Body and eat away at fellowship. These negatives divert the focus away from the Head of the Body and divert energies away from pursuing the mission. They also hurt people and drive them away.

The 12 Seeds can be used by any worshipping community – and by any team, group or small church within that community – as Biblically-based principles that build up the Body and strengthen it to be what the Lord calls it to be: a blessing for each member and a powerful witness to the world. When the Body is built up in this way, it is better able to pursue its mission and it is more attractive to visitors and new members.

GIFTS THAT FILL NEEDS

The 12 Seeds can be thought of as gifts to give others. These gifts don't require the use of cash or a credit card. They are thoughts, words and actions that can be given in any situation. They are useful gifts: they help fill needs. See the chart on page 113 for a list of the some of the needs that the seeds help fill.

LEARNING FOR A LIFETIME

It is wise to learn how to build and maintain good relationships. Such learning is part of the foundation to all other success in life. Whether you're a professional educator or not, training in the principles for successful relationships deserves ongoing attention. Such training is an investment for a lifetime.

AGENTS OF CHANGE

The twelve principles can also be thought of as ways to help transform a life, a relationship, a family, a team, a church, a business, or any other organization. The seeds can be effective agents of change that will make a profound difference in people's lives.

Substantive change usually takes time and effort. Though sometimes a new practice of a seed such as *appreciation* or *integrity* may have an immediate and dramatic effect, more often it requires ongoing planting and cultivating. But the harvest is well worth it. To make a difference, continue to plant and cultivate the seeds. People will be positively impacted. Try it!

Remember the saying, "Some people brighten a room when they walk in, others when they walk out." Be one who brightens the room when you walk in.

STEPS TOWARD RECONCILIATION

One of the most rewarding occurrences in life is reconciliation. Remember, *reconciliation is restoration of relationship.* If you've suffered a broken relationship, or know someone who has, you can use the seeds as steps toward reconciliation. Suggested ways to do this are given on page 118 in Part III of this book.

SEEDS OF GENERAL GOODWILL

The angels announced the birth of Christ with the words: "Glory to God in the highest, and on earth peace, good will toward men."Lk 2:14 KJV

When we look at the world today, at times we see very little goodwill toward men. But when we look at Christ, and study His life, we see Him always sharing goodwill toward others. Followers of Christ down through history have continued to share goodwill in many ways. They have fed the hungry and sheltered the homeless. They have engaged in famine relief, disaster recovery, and the building of schools, hospitals amd orphanages.

Whatever we do, or wherever we are, we can think of the 12 Seeds as some of the ways that our daily habits can blossom into lives of goodwill that bless many people.

SEEDS OF BUSINESS GOODWILL

When a healthy business is sold, *goodwill* is usually a major part of the valuation of the enterprise. In fact, the value of goodwill can actually exceed the value of the tangible assets.

Just how is goodwill created in a company? It's easy to assume that goodwill is simply the result of being in business for a period of time, or of avoiding any major public relations blunders. But the truth is that goodwill is the result of an intentional, ongoing commitment to principles and values that build long-term, mutually profitable relationships. Most every costly problem in business in-

"Just how is goodwill created in a company?"

volves the absence or weakness of one or more of these principles; most every success involves their presence.

The 12 Seeds are some of the principles and values that help build lasting goodwill with employees, customers, suppliers and others involved with the enterprise:

Employees: The principles contribute to a culture of teamwork that boosts morale, productivity and loyalty. They help provide one of the finest of all employee benefits: a positive, uplifting workplace environment. Practicing the 12 Seeds on the job can also yield highly desirable benefits for each employee at home. Also, a commitment to the twelve principles can help a firm achieve the highly desirable "Employer of Choice" status that attracts and keeps excellent employees.

Customers: The seeds provide the basis for a customer relations policy that yields long-term, mutually profitable relationships. The presence of these values influences customer buying decisions and contributes to the "plus value" that a quality business gives to the people it serves.

Suppliers and outside contractors: The seeds help build the cooperative, reliable relationships that are vital in this age of "just in time" delivery and outsourcing to trusted partners.

Others: The twelve principles help build confidence among shareholders, bankers and others. They give additional good reasons to be associated with the firm. They help build a quality reputation in the marketplace and in the community.

CORE VALUES

The core values of any family, friendship, group, team, business, church or community are foundational building blocks that guide present and future activities. They provide a basis for principled interaction among members of the group, and also between members and those outside the group. The 12 Seeds can be adopted as part of the core values of any values-oriented organization.

Why study the 12 Seeds?

Study and periodically review the seeds to:

- Grow in your relationship with the Lord.
- Grow in your relationships with others.
- Learn ways to improve your family life.
- Be more successful on the job.
- Build your business.
- Help your church grow.
- Be more of a blessing to other people.
- Learn ways to reconcile with someone.
- Be better able to spot the symptoms when one or more of the seeds is weak or missing.
- Avoid the painful costs of poor relationships.
- Learn ways to help transform the cultural environment where you live or work.
- Become a more effective leader.
- Remind yourself to practice the principles.
- Be better equipped to help others with their relationships – especially if you are a parent, grandparent, friend, coach, mentor or teacher.

Anticipate the Harvest

Expect transformational impact!

Seeds yield a harvest. The harvest could have life-changing impact upon you and upon everyone around you! The word *harvest* is defined as "the result or consequence of an activity." As you plant and cultivate the 12 Seeds, the harvest could yield dramatic results in the lives of many people.

Author John Maxwell states that the average person will influence 10,000 people in a lifetime. And Joe Girard, known as "the world's greatest salesperson," claims that the average person knows 250 other people. Therefore, if you know 250 people, and you positively influence them so that they in turn positively influence the 250 people they know, the potential number influenced becomes quite large: $250 \times 250 = 62,500$. If you're above average – and if you're reading

> "Imagine what the harvest might look like!"

this book we think of you as above average – then you may know far more than 250 people. The point is, your positive influence can favorably impact many people. Imagine what the harvest might look like:

> ***In your Family:*** A higher quality of living with more good words – *benedictions* – and more thoughtful acts of love; more enjoyable relationships all through life.

> ***In your Church:*** Members growing together in loving fellowship, meeting one another's needs; more involvement in mission; a more winsome outreach to your community.

On your Team or in your Group: Higher morale, co-operation and productivity; less focus on relational problems, more focus on reaching shared goals.

In your School: Students and teachers learning and practicing relationship principles together; strife decreasing, with learning in all subjects increasing.

In your Business or Profession: A better workplace environment, with more productive employees and more satisfied customers, with suppliers and contractors who know and support your values.

Wherever you are: More rewarding interpersonal involvements and more lasting friendships, with a decrease in the pain of poor relationships and an increase in the joy of good relationships.

PART OF THE HARVEST: FILLING NEEDS

The seeds help fill needs. When you say or do things that respect another person, for example, you are helping to fill their need for significance. The table below summarizes some of the needs that each seed helps fill:

THE SEED	THE NEED IT HELPS FILL
RESPECT	significance
ENCOURAGEMENT	courage to press on
LISTENING	attention
APPRECIATION	to be valued
TRUST	security
INTEGRITY	authenticity
ORDER	structure
NURTURE	to be loved
SYNERGY	to work together
HOPE	motivation to go on
IDEALS	to focus on higher things
PARDON	forgiveness

"Now He who supplies seed to the sower and bread for food will also supply and increase your store of seed and will enlarge the harvest of your righteousness."

II Corinthians 9:10

RESPECT
ENCOURAGEMENT
LISTENING
APPRECIATION
TRUST
INTEGRITY
ORDER
NURTURE
SYNERGY
HOPE
IDEALS
PARDON

PART III

Resources for a Rich Harvest

Abundant Living in Successful Relationships

Your Most Important Relationship in Life

You may have read to this point and seen references in this book to a personal relationship with the Lord Jesus Christ. Hopefully you already enjoy such a relationship. Or, you may wonder, *just how does a person come into a personal relationship with the Lord?*

People who are in such a relationship consider it the most important thing in life. It's more than just a part of life. It *is* life.

The significance of this relationship has prompted many followers of Jesus Christ, when describing Christianity, to say, "It's not a religion. It's a relationship!" It is the one relationship that makes a dramatic difference

The Perfect Friend

He had regard – RESPECT – for His creation
when He came to live among us and redeem us.

He gives us ENCOURAGEMENT, and He LISTENS to us!

He values – APPRECIATES – people. He TRUSTS
His Father, and He entrusts us to do His work on earth.

He is the perfect example of INTEGRITY.

He gives ORDER to life, and He NURTURES us.

There's a beautiful SYNERGY as we work together
with His Spirit and with others who follow Him.

He is our HOPE, and He enables us to share hope with others.

He displays, and is, the very highest of IDEALS.

He graciously offers us PARDON!

His Name is JESUS. He is the Head of the Body.
He is the Resurrection and the Life! Praise Him forever!
What a joy to be in an everlasting RELATIONSHIP with Him!

What a privilege to know Him and
share His love with others!

– a follower of Jesus

in all other relationships in life. In fact, it affects every aspect of life, for now and for eternity. Don't miss out!

Even though some of the people who enjoy such a relationship may not tell you about it, those who truly love you want you to know, because love is "seeking the highest welfare of the one loved." What could be a higher welfare than a relationship with the living God, who came to us in the person of Jesus? He gives us eternal, abundant life with Him!

In the "seed chapters" in Part I of this book, you've already learned something about twelve facets of a relationship with the Lord. However, the Bible teaches that before we can have a right relationship with God, we need to be reconciled to Him. Our sins separate us from Him. We need His forgiveness.

The Good News is that God offers us a way to be forgiven and reconciled to Him. Jesus Christ provides the way. In fact, He *is* the Way. When we come to know Him, we find that He is also the Truth and the Life.

Four steps to a personal relationship with the Lord Jesus Christ:

   1. ADMIT – that you are a sinner, and need a Savior.
   2. REPENT – be willing to turn from your sins.
   3. BELIEVE – that Jesus died for you on the Cross.
   4. RECEIVE – invite, through prayer, Jesus Christ
      to come into your heart to be Lord of your life.

What to Pray

Dear Lord Jesus, I know that I am a sinner. I need Your forgiveness. I believe that You died for my sins. I want to turn from my sins. I now invite You to come into my heart and life. I want to trust and follow You as Savior and Lord. In Your Name, Amen.

References: Proverbs 14:12; Isaiah 59:2; John 1:12, 3:16, 10:10, 14:6;
Romans 3:23, 5:1, 5:8, 6:23, 10:9, 10:13; II Corinthians 5:17-21;
Colossians 1:15-22; I Peter 2:24, 3:18; I John 1:9; 5:11-13; Revelation 3:20

Steps Toward Healing a Relationship

A pathway toward reconciliation with another person

Relationships can become strained or broken. Weeds can invade. Sometimes strengthening just one or two seeds may help. The following steps can be used to start toward healing and reconciliation.

> **"Reconciliation is restoration of relationship."**

1. Pray for the welfare of the other person.

2. Pray for help in seeing which seed(s) are weak or missing in your relationship. *Ask yourself, in prayer before the Lord (put the person's name in the blanks):*

   "Do I *respect* _____?"
   "Do I *encourage* _____?"
   "Do I *listen* to _____?"
   "Do I *appreciate* _____?"
   "Do I *trust* _____? Am I trustworthy with _____?"
   "Do I practice *integrity* with _____?"

   Continue through the 12 seeds, thinking of the other person in relation to each seed.

3. Pray for wisdom to identify the seed(s) you need to cultivate in your own life, especially in this relationship.

4. Restudy the chapter on the seed(s) identified in Step 3, above. Select specific Prayers, Thoughts, Words and Actions you'll practice as you relate to the other person.

5. Pray for help in cultivating the seed(s). Put the person's name in a prayer about that seed. Example: *Lord, help me to treat _____ with dignity and respect.*

6. Don't wait for the *other* person to change before *you* will start taking these steps. Don't even expect them to act differently *after* you start taking these steps. *But they may!*

7. *Do* expect a change in how *you* think and act toward the other person as you prayerfully take these steps.

These steps can also be used to make a good relationship even better!

A Powerful Growth Formula
Virtues that help relationships grow

The Bible contains many verses that give guidance for relationships. In the passage below Paul gives us a powerful "growth formula" that can help relationships grow and flourish.

> **Therefore, as God's chosen people, holy and dearly loved, clothe yourselves with compassion, kindness, humility, gentleness and patience. Bear with each other and forgive whatever grievances you may have against one another. Forgive as the Lord forgave you. And over all these virtues put on love, which binds them all together in perfect unity.**
>
> – Colossians 3:12-14

We could state the formula this way:

L+CKHGP = Growing Relationships

Here's an explanation:

L = LOVE

The last sentence in the above passage says, "over all these virtues put on love, which binds them all together in perfect unity." A good working definition for love is "seeking the highest welfare of the one loved." Love is the motivation for planting and cultivating the 12 Seeds. It's also the bonding agent, the glue that holds good relationships together. The word *love* is used 551 times in the Bible.

> **"Love is the motivation for planting and cultivating the 12 Seeds."**

C = COMPASSION

Compassion is sympathy moved to action. It is a deep awareness of the need or suffering of another, together with the desire to relieve it. Each of the 12 Seeds is a way to help meet the needs of others. There may be a need in a person's life for a seed of respect, or encouragement, or hope. Seeds help fill needs. The word *compassion* is used 77 times in the Bible.

> **"Seeds help fill needs."**

K = KINDNESS

Kindness has to do with being friendly, generous, tender, warm-hearted, agreeable. Seeds flourish in the warmth of kindness. The Bible says something very interesting about kindness in responding to people who have needs: "He who is kind to the poor lends to the LORD, and He will reward him for what he has done." [Pr 19:17] The word *kindness* is used 65 times in the Bible.

> **"Seeds flourish in the warmth of kindness."**

H = HUMILITY

Humility is meekness or modesty in behavior or spirit. It is the opposite of pride and arrogance. The word *humility* is from the Latin *humilis*, which means low or lowly, and *humus*, which means ground or soil. Just as biological seeds grow in the soil of the earth, the 12 Seeds grow in the soil of humility. The word *humility* is used 14 times in the Bible, the word *humble* is used 40 times.

> **"The 12 Seeds grow in the soil of humility."**

C.S. Lewis has a beautiful statement about humility in his beloved book, *Mere Christianity:* "Do not imagine that if you meet a really humble man he will be what most people call 'humble' nowadays: he will not be a sort of greasy, smarmy person, who is always telling you that, of course, he is nobody. Probably all you will think about him is that he seemed a cheerful, intelligent chap who took a real interest in what *you* said to *him*. If you do dislike him it will be because you feel a little envious of anyone who seems to enjoy life so easily. He will not be thinking about humility: he will not be thinking about himself at all."

G = GENTLENESS

Gentleness is being considerate and amiable, the opposite of being harsh or severe. A gentle person has the capacity to be otherwise, but instead is mild and tender. Gentleness is truth and strength guided by love. Seeds thrive in gentle climates. The word *gentleness* is used 6 times in the Bible, the word *gentle* is used 18 times.

"Seeds thrive in gentle climates."

P = PATIENCE

Patience is bearing pain, difficulty or annoyance with an enduring and calm spirit. The passage also uses the phrase "bear with one another," a reference to forbearance, which is restraint in the face of provocation. Forbearance is related to patience, and has been called "patience under pressure." Patience involves an investment of time. Seeds take time to grow. The harvest will be some time in the future. The word *patience* is used 17 times in the Bible, the word *patient* is used 19 times.

"Seeds take time to grow."

L+CKHGP = Growing Relationships

Use the "growth formula" in your practice of the 12 Seeds!

 **Verses to Plant in Your Mind**

Theme verses from the start of each "seed chapter"
in Part I, to plant and cultivate in your mind!

RESPECT

**Honor one another
above yourselves.**
– Romans 12:10 NIV

ENCOURAGEMENT

**Let us not give up meeting
together, as some are in
the habit of doing, but let
us encourage one another
– and all the more as you
see the Day approaching.**
– Hebrews 10:25

LISTENING

**Everyone should be quick
to listen, slow to speak
and slow to become angry.**
– James 1:19b

APPRECIATION

**Be joyful always; pray
continually; give thanks
in all circumstances, for
this is God's will for
you in Christ Jesus.**
– 1 Thessalonians 5:16-18

TRUST

**Trust in the LORD
with all your heart and
lean not on your own
understanding; in all your
ways acknowledge Him,
and He will make your
paths straight.**
– Proverbs 3:5-6

INTEGRITY

**The integrity of the
upright guides them,
but the unfaithful
are destroyed by
their duplicity.**
– Proverbs 11:3

ORDER

**Everything should be
done in a fitting
and orderly way.**
– 1 Corinthians 14:40

NURTURE

Love never fails.
– 1 Corinthians 13:8a

SYNERGY

**Now you are the body of
Christ, and each one of you
is a part of it.**
– 1 Corinthians 12:27

HOPE

**May the God of hope fill
you with all joy and peace
as you trust in Him, so that
you may overflow with
hope by the power
of the Holy Spirit.**
– Romans 15:13

IDEALS

**Whatever is true, whatever
is noble, whatever is right,
whatever is pure, whatever
is lovely, whatever is
admirable –
if anything is excellent
or praiseworthy –
think about such things.**
– Philippians 4:8

PARDON

**Bear with each other
and forgive whatever
grievances you may have
against one another.
Forgive as the Lord
forgave you.**
– Colossians 3:13

The Prayer of a Relationship-Builder

Dear Lord, please help me to treat others with dignity and **respect**. Help me to **encourage, listen, appreciate** and **trust**.

Help me to live with the **integrity** and **order** that is a blessing to others. Prompt me to **nurture** as needed, and give me the cooperative spirit that allows **synergy** to flourish.

Grant me the well-spring of **hope** and the treasure of **ideals**. And remind me, when others fail to exhibit the above qualities, to **pardon** them as You have pardoned me.

Thank You, Lord, for relationships. May the way I relate to others be a refreshing witness of the life-changing relationship I have with You.

How to Use this Book for Personal Growth
A suggested curriculum for personal development

Level 1: Read this book – highlight the parts most meaningful to you, and think of specific people in your life. Pray for wisdom to identify the seed(s) you're strong in, and also which seeds you need to grow.

Level 2: Memorize the Relationship Acrostic (see page 87). Have a friend test you on it.

Level 3: Review the 12 Seeds periodically to refresh them in your mind, and to be better equipped to help others understand and practice them.

Level 4: Memorize the "working definitions" for each seed – these definitions are given at the start of each chapter, under the name of the seed. They're also summarized on the "Bad Seeds/Good Seeds" chart on page 93.

Level 5: Review the Practical Applications for the seed(s) you need to grow. Circle or highlight the suggested items you'll commit to work on.

Level 6: Memorize the theme Bible verse for each seed – the theme verse is at the start of each seed chapter.

Level 7: Meditate upon the verses listed in "Practical Applications" – a good thing to do during personal devotions or quiet time. If possible, look the verse up in more than one Bible translation.

Level 8: Practice the seeds – in a general sense with everyone; in specific applications with specific people.

Level 9: Ask a friend to hold you accountable to practice the seeds, or to practicing specific applications.

Level 10: Watch for people practicing any of the 12 Seeds – encourage them – seek to promote a cultural environment in which the seeds and relationships grow.

**For more ideas on how to use this book personally
or in a group, please visit: www.12seeds.com**

How to Use this Book in a Class or Group
Suggested agenda ideas

NOTE: Allow at least 30-60 minutes to discuss each seed when going through the book for the first time. We recommend that each person read a chapter before discussing it.

1. Open in prayer. There are suggestions for prayers in the Practical Applications section of each seed chapter.

2. Review the 12 Seeds RELATIONSHIP acrostic together. Also, review the seed studied in the previous session. Ask for any added insights or experiences since last session, or any observances of the seed being practiced.

3. Have one person read the first section of the chapter aloud. Discuss briefly.

4. Continue through the chapter, rotating the reading of the text among different people. Discuss briefly.

5. In the Practical Applications section, ask volunteers to lead in one or more of the suggested prayers. Then, ask different people to look up the suggested Scriptures. Have each person read their verse aloud, in succession. Then, ask each reader to reread their respective verse. Discuss briefly. Discuss the suggested thoughts, words and actions. Share personal experiences, insights and additional applications.

6. Discuss the suggested questions.

7. Close in prayer.

> **Expect a high level of participation in a 12 Seeds discussion!**

Advanced ideas: Encourage each participant to use the personal growth suggestions on the page at left. Recite the 12 Seeds acrostic together from memory in your sessions. Quiz one another on the various seeds, and their meanings. Adopt the seeds as standards for your group, with a goal of creating a cultural environment that promotes the growth of all the seeds. Establish accountability relationships; invite participants to report on progress made.

Multiply the impact: Revisit the 12 Seeds periodically, sharing new insights and experiences. Add a regular agenda item to your regular weekly or monthly meeting: briefly review one seed each meeting. This refreshes memories and also helps orient new members to your values. Visit: www.12seeds.com for more ideas.

Acknowledgements

First of all, we want to acknowledge the Lord. He created us, and He created relationships. He seeks a closer relationship with each one of us, and He teaches us how to relate to others. This book is dedicated to Him.

We also want to thank all the people the Lord has used to help make this book possible. They have prayed for this book, and for you the reader. They have also offered creative ideas, constructive criticism, editing help, encouragement and financing. We have seen these folks practice all 12 Seeds as they have helped on this book.

Thanks also to the people who have used 12 Seeds materials since we first started publishing them in early 2000. We've learned much from those of you who have been using the materials in your homes, workplaces and churches. A number of your suggestions are incorporated into this revised and expanded edition.

Compiling this book has been a great experience in relationships. We are thankful for all who have helped, and for the privilege of seeing many relationships, including our own, grow in the process.

ADDITIONAL RESOURCES AVAILABLE ON OUR WEBSITE

You'll find materials you can download for free, such as . . .

- The 12 Seeds Leader-Mentor Guide (latest version)
- The GROW ONE Personal Seedgrowing Guide
- Bookmarks displaying the RELATIONSHIP acrostic
- Promotional materials you can use to help invite people to a 12 Seeds class or discussion group you conduct

You'll also find Questions & Answers about the 12 Seeds, 50 Reasons to plant the seeds, plus additional ideas.

Visit our website at:

www.12seeds.com

The 12 Seeds, when planted and cultivated, yield harvests that benefit individuals, families, groups, teams, schools, churches, businesses, communities and all of society.

12 Seeds materials are increasingly being used in prisons, released offender ministry and addiction recovery. To find out more about this, email us at: info@12seeds.com

---

Send us your comments, insights and experiences! We love to hear about how the 12 Seeds are being used, and the harvests they're helping to produce! Also, tell us how we can improve our materials to serve you better. Your suggestions are always welcome. Email us at: comments@12seeds.com

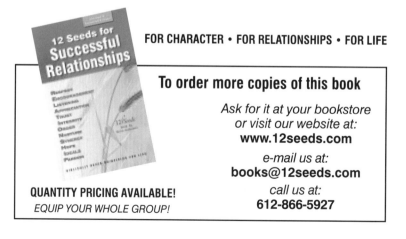

FOR CHARACTER • FOR RELATIONSHIPS • FOR LIFE

To order more copies of this book

*Ask for it at your bookstore
or visit our website at:*
www.12seeds.com

e-mail us at:
books@12seeds.com

call us at:
612-866-5927

QUANTITY PRICING AVAILABLE!
EQUIP YOUR WHOLE GROUP!

"The good life? We do not experience it in the loneliness of today's fads of self-expression and self-gratification. The good life is found only in loving relationships and community."

– Chuck Colson, *The Good Life*